THE MUSIC KIT

THE MUSIC KIT

THIRD EDITION

TOM MANOFF

Computer Programs by   JOHN MILLER, *The University of North Dakota*

PETER HESTERMAN, *Eastern Illinois University*

with TOM MANOFF

Workbook

W · W · NORTON & COMPANY · New York · London

Third Edition

The text of this book is composed in Optima
Composition by David Budmen, Willow Graphics, Woodstown, NJ
Manufacturing by Courier, Westford
Book design by Jack Meserole

Library of Congress Cataloging-in-Publication Data

Manoff, Tom.
    The music kit / Tom Manoff ; computer programs by John Miller and Peter Hesterman,
    with Tom Manoff. — 3rd ed.
        p.   cm.
    ISBN 0-393-96325-X
    1. Music—Theory, Elementary.   I. Title.
MT7.M267   1994
781.2—dc20   94-39433
                                    CIP
                                    MN

ISBN 0-393-96325-X   0-393-96327-6 (Apple II)   0-393-96330-6 (Macintosh)

W. W. Norton & Company, Inc., 500 Fifth Avenue, New York, N.Y. 10110
W. W. Norton & Company Ltd., 10 Coptic Street, London WC1A 1PU

    2   3   4   5   6   7   8   9   0

Contents

Preface to the Third Edition ix

CHAPTER ONE   1

Notation   1
Pitch   1
The Notation of Pitch   1
Music Handwriting   2
Note Names   3
The Octave   4
Note Names on the Staff   5
The Treble Clef   5
Notes in the Treble Clef   6

The Bass Clef   7
Notes in the Bass Clef   7
Ledger Lines   8
Writing Ledger Lines   9
The Grand Staff   10
Middle C   10
Learning Note Names   10
Terms, Symbols, and Concepts   21
Suggested Activities   21

CHAPTER TWO   22

The Piano Keyboard   22
Other Keyboards   22
The Design of the Keyboard   22
The White Keys   22
The Black Keys   24

Enharmonic Spelling   24
Notating the White Keys   27
Notating the Black Keys   30
Terms, Symbols, and Concepts   32
Suggested Activities   32

CHAPTER THREE   33

Half Steps and Whole Steps   33
Half Steps   33
Whole Steps   34
Semitone and Whole Tone   35
Semitone Types   35
Accidentals   38

Accidentals in a Measure   41
Use of the Natural   41
Precautionary Accidentals   41
Visualizing a Keyboard   44
Terms, Symbols, and Concepts   44
Suggested Activities   44

CHAPTER FOUR   45

Scales   45
Diatonic Scales   45
The Major Scale   46
Building a Major Scale on D   48
Adding Accidentals to Form a Major
    Scale   48
The Importance of Correct Spelling   49
Major-Scale Spellings   50
"In the Key of"   53

Tonality   53
Melody   55
Intervals   55
Melodic and Harmonic Intervals   57
Melody and Intervals   59
Inversion   60
Terms, Symbols, and Concepts   61
Suggested Activities   62

CHAPTER FIVE 63

Key Signatures   63
Adding a Key Signature   64
Organization of Major-Scale Key
   Signatures   68
The Circle of 5ths   69
Transposition   71
Transposing Accidentals   74
Chromatic and Diatonic   76
Melodic Organization   77

Phrase and Form   77
Words and Music   77
The Cadence   78
Melodic Shape   78
Composing a Melody   80
Singing Major-Scale Melodies   82
Terms, Symbols, and Concepts   82
Suggested Activities   83

CHAPTER SIX 84

Intervals   84
Staff Steps and Half Steps   84
Interval Quality   86
Intervals within the Major Scale   89
Altering Major-Scale Intervals   91
Limitations of the Major-Scale
   Method   94
The Natural Semitones   94

The Natural Intervals   95
Adding Accidentals   97
Quality of Inverted Intervals   100
Other Applications of Diminished and
   Augmented   100
Consonance and Dissonance   101
Terms, Symbols, and Concepts   103
Suggested Activities   103

CHAPTER SEVEN 104

The Minor Scale   104
Natural Minor Scale Construction   104
Minor-Scale Key Signatures   107
Relative Minor/Relative Major   108
Finding the Relative Minor Scale   109
Finding the Relative Major Scale   109
Minor-Scale Key Signatures/Circle
   of 5ths   110
Parallel Minor/Parallel Major   113
The Relationship of Parallel Major to
   Minor   114

Singing the Natural Minor Scale   115
Other Forms of the Minor Scale   115
The Harmonic Minor Scale   116
The Augmented 2nd   117
The Melodic Minor Scale   120
Minor Scales and Musical Usage   123
The Chromatic Scale   124
Terms, Symbols, and Concepts   125
Suggested Activities   125

CHAPTER EIGHT 127

Harmony and Chords   127
Triads   127
Quality of Triads   128
Triads and Scales   128
Working with Triads   132
Learning the Triads   133
Triads on B and B♭   134
Voicing   136
Voicing for Four-Part Chorus   136
Chord Inversions   138
Harmonic Background of a Melody   139

Harmonic Progression   140
Composing a Chord Melody   141
Nonchord Tones   142
Neighbor Tones   142
Passing Tones   143
Notating Voices: Various Methods   144
Harmonizing a Melody with 3rds
   and 6ths   145
Canons and Rounds   146
Terms, Symbols, and Concepts   147
Suggested Activities   147

CHAPTER NINE   149

Complex Triad Spellings   149
An Aid for Spelling Other Triads   150
Diminished and Augmented Triads   152
Altering Triads   152
The Harmonic System   154
Transposing Chords   159
Motive   160

Rhythmic Identity of a Motive   160
Pitch Identity of a Motive   161
Sequence   162
Inversion   163
Motivic Development   163
Terms, Symbols, and Concepts   166
Suggested Activities   166

CHAPTER TEN   168

7th Chords   168
7th-Chord Quality   168
The Dominant 7th Chord   169
Complex Spelling of 7th Chords   173
Minor-Scale Triads: Position in Key   174
V or V^7 in a Minor Key   175

The Minor 7th Chord   178
The Major 7th Chord   179
Diminished and Half-Diminished 7th
   Chords   181
Terms, Symbols, and Concepts   183
Suggested Activities   183

CHAPTER ELEVEN   184

Accompaniments to Melodies   184
Keyboard Accompaniments   184
Voice Leading   185
Common Tone   186
Voicing the V^7 187
Voicing V^7 in a Minor Key   188
Adding the Bass   188
Additional Voicings of I, IV, and V^7 189
Using V Instead of V^7 192

Harmonizing with the vi Chord   194
Harmonizing with the ii Chord   195
Tonality and the V or V^7 196
Modulation   196
How to Harmonize a Melody   197
Parallelism in Modern Accompaniments   197
Voice Leading in Popular Styles   198
Terms, Symbols, and Concepts   200
Suggested Activities   200

CHAPTER TWELVE   202

Modes   202
Scale and Mode Mixture   207
Pentatonic Scale   208
Form: Phrase Design   209
The Period   210
Two Types of Cadences   210
Melodic Aspects of Cadential Design   210
Double Period   211
The Design of Phrase Forms   211

Labeling Phrases   212
Parallel and Contrasting Periods   213
The Three-Phrase Period   214
Flexibility of Form Designations   214
A Summary of Melodic Design   214
Composing Melodies   214
Terms, Symbols, and Concepts   217
Suggested Activities   217

REVIEW EXERCISES   218

Appendixes   236

I. Checklist of Notation Symbols   236
II. Major and Minor Scales and Key
   Signatures   238
III. Methods of Sight Singing   240
IV. Triads and Chords   241
V. Progressions for Improvisation and
   Composition   243

VI. How to Read a Lead Sheet   246
VII. The Guitar Fretboard and Guitar
   Chords   250
VIII. Recorder Fingering   252
IX. Harmonic Series   253
X. Glossary of Terms   254

Preface to the Third Edition

New Features

The third edition of *The Music Kit* builds on many years of success in the college classroom. While there has been no radical departure from past editions, certain features have been expanded, and new material and music have been added. These enhancements owe much to the valuable advice and requests from longtime users of the book. Changes notwithstanding, the original objectives and procedures of the text remain intact.

Philosophy and Approach

The Music Kit was written for the beginning student of musicianship. Unlike some topics of study, musicianship embraces much more than factual information. It requires a variety of skills and concepts that allow the musician to negotiate the many facets of understanding and making music as a composer and performer. To that end, *The Music Kit* offers a practical, step-by-step presentation to attain a high level of musicianship. Having completed this book successfully, the student will be thoroughly prepared for further study in the theory of music or for amateur music making.

A brief examination of the chapter headings reveals the traditional topics of music fundamentals. But there are underlying threads that this bird's-eye view does not reveal. Musicians learn through a variety of approaches at once. Here, certain material is considered from several viewpoints. Factual information, skills, and concepts are presented in layers throughout the book, each new layer building on and interwoven with the previous one. Thus, the first three chapters not only teach note names and the keyboard but also introduce the skills and concepts that enable the student to become fluent in reading the staff; Chapters Four and Five not only teach key signatures but also present several vital concepts that explain the inner working of our musical system and thus why key signatures exist. And perhaps most important, several chapters include the study of melody in the context of our Western system of tonality, with the aim of enabling the student to compose by the time the book is finished.

Scope of The Music Kit

The Music Kit, third edition, is comprised of several parts: the *Workbook*, the *Rhythm Reader and Scorebook*, and the cassette tape. (Students with one of the computer versions, whose exercises correspond to and extend those in the texts, may refer to the computer documentation for additional information.) The *Workbook* presents the main tasks of the course. The student literally "works" through this text—reading, listening, performing, and responding to the short tutorials and exercises. *The Music Kit* is a "hands-on" book. The reader should have a pencil in hand at all times, since few pages will go by without a request to work through a concept or to begin to write music.

Workbook

Divided into twelve chapters plus a review section, the *Workbook* has several features that offer flexibility in learning the material. At the end of each chapter are two important sections. The first, called "Terms, Symbols, and Concepts," includes the basic topics and ideas presented in the chapter. Defining and explaining each of these will lead to mastery of the material. The reader might first think about each term from memory, then use both the text and the Glossary at the end of the book to formally write out the definitions. As she proceeds through the text, checking back to these sections from time to time will help keep these ideas fine-tuned and in her mind. The second section, called "Suggested Activities," provides a wide range of additional work. Designed to extend and explore the concepts of each chapter, these exercises allow the reader to refine and more thoroughly apply the material of each chapter to his growing mastery of musicianship. The material in the "Suggested Activities" sections may be postponed until a later date—when the student can go through it at a more leisurely pace—if he is taking a course in a short period of time.

Rhythm Reader

The *Rhythm Reader* is a companion volume to the *Workbook*. Much shorter and dealing only with rhythm, its twelve chapters should be studied at the same time as the *Workbook*. The exercises in the *Rhythm Reader* are based on recorded rhythms found on the cassette tape. Learning these rhythms is essential for working through this short study. While the recorded rhythms may seem easy at first, they become more difficult and interesting as the student proceeds. An appendix of empty grids, called Rhythm Spacers—a visual device to help understand rhythmic notation—is given at the end of the *Rhythm Reader*. These Rhythm Spacers can serve to notate additional music examples provided by the student or instructor.

Scorebook

The *Scorebook*, a collection of melodies (some with harmony) that are referred to in both the *Workbook* and the *Rhythm Reader*, is at the center of *The Music Kit*. The *Scorebook* presents examples from a variety of musical repertories to demonstrate the various elements covered in the text. It consists of four sections. (1) "Melodies from Around the World": supplied without words so that the reader can focus purely on musical structure, these melodies are drawn from the traditional music of many countries; (2) "Songs and Ballads": furnished with words, these pieces demonstrate the many ways music and text are joined together; (3) "Canons, Rounds, and Part Songs": these pieces are meant to be sung by a group; and (4) "From the Classical Heritage": except for a few examples, the melodies in this section are short excerpts from longer pieces. All four sections follow a graduated plan; the level of musical difficulty increases toward the end of each section. The various levels are intended to meet the wide range of musical experience found in the college classroom. Indeed, some pieces may require extra effort or help from the instructor to understand.

Cassette Tape

The cassette tape offers two kinds of selections: (1) forty-four rhythmic exercises and (2) six pieces from the *Scorebook*.

Side One	*Side Two*
Rhythms 1–12	Rhythms 24–35
Rhythms 13–23	Rhythms 36–44
I Know Where I'm Going	*Dear Willie*
The Water is Wide	*En el portal de Belén*
Greensleeves	

The rhythmic exercises are numbered and are introduced by number on the cassette. While the pieces from the *Scorebook* are not announced on the cassette tape, they are printed on the cassette itself. The reader is strongly advised to become familiar with the contents of the cassette tape before beginning to work through *The Music Kit*. This will prevent unnecessary confusion when asked to listen to a particular example.

Performing the Examples

Throughout the *Workbook* and *Rhythm Reader* are music examples that, depending on the reader's background, she may be able to play on a piano or other keyboard instrument. I highly encourage this practice. Or the reader can sing the examples, perhaps with the help of the instructor. While singing seems to be disappearing from our culture (many students feel embarrassed to sing), it is a simple truth that singing music is the best way to absorb, experience, and understand musical structure. Trained musicians are in the habit of singing any piece of music that passes in front of their eyes.

Acknowledgements

I have many people to thank for their contributions to the third edition of *The Music Kit*. Invaluable suggestions were received from each of the following: Kevin Blatchford (Phoenix College), William Carson (Coe College), John Floreen (Rutgers University, Newark), Randi L'Hommedieu (Mississippi State University), Mark Scatterday (Cornell University), John Specht (Queensborough Community College), David Taylor (Ricks College), and Jeffrey Stolet (University of Oregon). Additional comments were provided by John Boden (University of Southern Maine, Gorham) and Rick Spitz (Cerritos College). The creation of the computer programs was made possible by a hardworking collaboration with John Miller and Peter Hesterman, with additional help from Philip Baczewski (University of North Texas) and Jane Clendinning (Florida State University). With original guidance from Raymond Morse, we could not have finished our task without the leadership of Stephen King of W. W. Norton. Also at Norton I extend my deepest thanks to Suzanne La Plante for her many hours of hard work revising and editing the manuscript and to Susan Gaustad for her suggestions. Most of all I thank my wife Milagro for listening to the words "next time it will be different."

Workbook

CHAPTER ONE

Notation

Music and language have some things in common. Both, for example, can be heard by the ear when played or spoken and seen by the eye when represented on the page. The printed words that you see here are one way of representing spoken language on the page. Another way is handwriting. Likewise, printed **notation** is one way to represent music on the page. Another way is **notating** it by hand. Letters are the basic symbols for writing language. **Notes** are the basic symbols for writing music. A musician can say, "I am writing music" or "I am notating music." Both are correct. **Note**, **notating**, **notation**—all are means by which musical sound is represented on a page.

Pitch

Have you ever noticed that a musical sound may seem either "high" or "low"? This aspect of music is **pitch**. Women, for example, can sing higher in pitch than men. The keys on the left side of a piano keyboard produce lower pitches than the keys on the right side. Another word sometimes used to describe pitch is **tone**, but pitch is the preferred term. (Compare both terms in the Glossary on p. 257–58.) When a pitch is written, it becomes a note.

The Notation of Pitch

Pitch is indicated by its position on a group of five lines called the **staff**.

STAFF

Notes are written either on the lines or in the spaces of the staff.

notes on lines   notes in spaces

 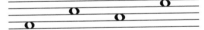

The higher a note is placed on the staff, the higher the pitch; the lower a note is placed on the staff, the lower the pitch. The direction of pitch from low to high is:

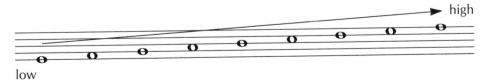

The direction of pitch from high to low is:

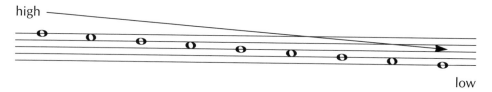

Music Handwriting

Handwritten musical notation, while rarely looking exactly like printed notation, should nevertheless be completely legible. Without demanding undue levels of uniformity, since no two people notate music in exactly the same manner, we can consider some basic rules of handwritten notation (see also *Rhythm Reader*, pp. 1 and 34–35):

1. The most important requirement of notation is legibility.
2. The notehead must single out a particular line or space clearly in order to identify a specific pitch.
3. A slightly oblong rather than round shape for the notehead works best. You will often find the notehead slanted higher to the right side.

Variations in the way you notate music will occur naturally as your skills and personal style develop.

1 Practice writing notes on lines and spaces as indicated.*

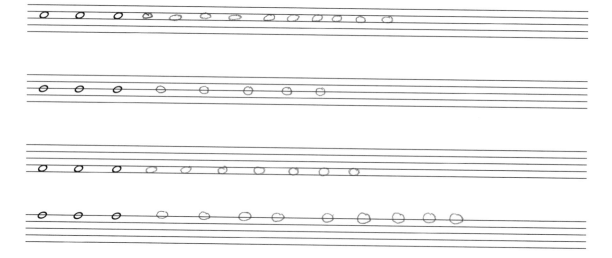

* You may wish to consult George Heussenstamm, *The Norton Manual of Music Notation* (New York: W.W. Norton, 1987) for further instructions on how to notate the various musical symbols.

2 Circle the lower note of each group. Notice that these notes are not handwritten, but are printed.

3 Circle the note in each group whose pitch lies *between* the other two. Study the example carefully.

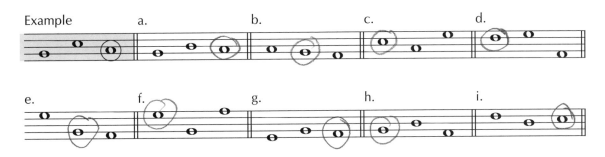

4 After the first two notes of each group, write a note whose pitch lies *between* the previous two. Take care to write legibly. There may be more than one correct answer for each group.

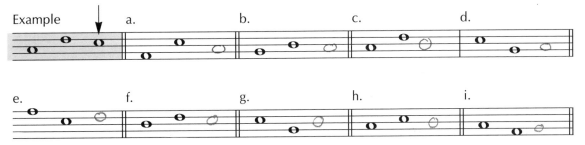

Note Names   The notes on a staff have the same names as the first seven letters of the alphabet. After G, we start with A again. From low to high:

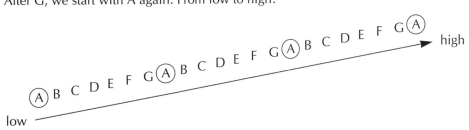

5   Starting from A. write the consecutive letter names of the notes, but with the pitch direction from high to low.

(A) G F E D C B (A) G F E D C B (A) G F E D C B (A) G F E D C B (A)

high ⟶

⟶ low

The Octave

Having moved both up and down through the pitch range, you may wonder about the repetition of note names. How can the same pitch exist at higher and lower levels? The answer lies in the physics of sound, a topic discussed in more detail in Appendix IX, "Harmonic Series," on page 253. The present demonstration serves as an introduction to that section.

Pluck any string on a guitar or other stringed instrument. Notice that the string vibrates. Listen to the pitch you've produced. Now divide the string exactly in half (on the guitar this is accomplished by pressing a finger on the twelfth fret). Compare this tone with the first. What you experience are two pitches that seem "different but the same." The pitches are an **octave** apart. Dividing the string exactly in half *doubles* the rate of vibration. Both pitches belong to a greater *class* of pitch. In this class, all pitches that are an octave apart have the same letter name; each pitch has double the vibrations of the pitch an octave below. For example, consider the pitch A, which vibrates 440 times per second. It belongs to the greater class of A's, which vibrate 220, 440, 880, etc., times per second. One octave above an A is another A. One octave below an F is another F. We speak of different octaves of the same pitch as being in higher or lower **registers**, or specific areas of the entire range of pitches available to an instrument or voice.

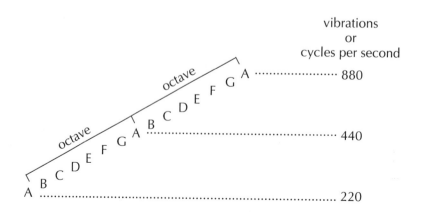

vibrations
or
cycles per second
·········· 880

·········· 440

·········· 220

Note Names on the Staff

Alternating lines and spaces on the staff indicate consecutive letter names of pitches. Thus, ascending in pitch:

If this line is E,   the next space is F,   the next line is G,   the next space is A.

E   F   G   A

And descending in pitch:

If this line is A,   the next space is G,   the next line is F,   the next space is E.

A   G   F   E

NAMING LINES AND SPACES

Consecutive letter names going up or down in pitch always appear as alternations between lines and spaces. The sequence may begin on a line or a space; for example, line-space-line-space or space-line-space-line.

The Treble Clef

Because there is not enough room on one staff to notate the pitches in all the registers, separate **staves** (the plural of staff) are used for high notes and low notes. A staff with a **treble clef** is used to notate high notes. This symbol indicates that the second line from the bottom on the staff is G. Because it identifies G, this clef is also called the **G clef**.

TREBLE CLEF OR G CLEF

6 Draw treble clefs in the manner shown in the example. Make sure that the loop wraps around the second line. Your hand-drawn clef will be an important element in your musical handwriting.

Notes in the Treble Clef

Learning to read notes requires practice. Study the note names in the treble clef as follows.

1. Consecutive letter names:

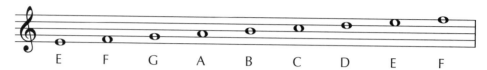

E   F   G   A   B   C   D   E   F

2. Names of lines:

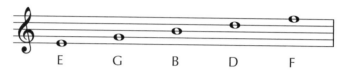

E   G   B   D   F

3. Names of spaces:

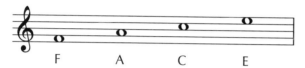

F   A   C   E

7   Identify each note. Notice that E and F each occur twice, in higher and lower octaves.

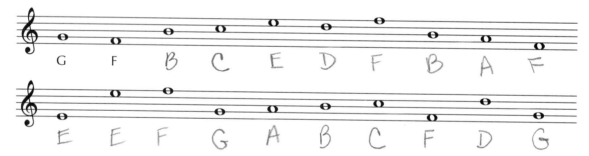

G   F   B   C   E   D   F   B   A   F

E   E   F   G   A   B   C   F   D   G

8   Write the indicated notes (use o). Make sure that each note falls directly on a line or a space. The first time E and F appear, write them in the higher octave, the second time in the lower octave.

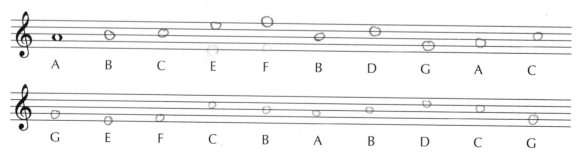

A   B   C   E   F   B   D   G   A   C

G   E   F   C   B   A   B   D   C   G

The Bass Clef

To notate low notes, we use the **bass clef**. It indicates that the second line from the top of the staff is F. The bass clef is also called the **F clef**.

Bass clef or F clef

9 The bass clef is easier to write than the treble clef. Draw several bass clefs, making the loop in one motion first, then adding the two dots. Make sure the loop and dots surround the F line.

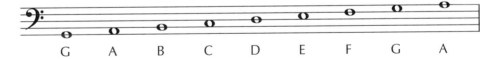

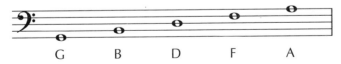

Notes in the Bass Clef

Study the notes in the bass clef as follows.

1. Consecutive letter names:

2. Names of lines:

3. Names of spaces:

10 Identify each note.

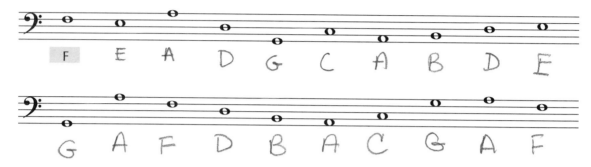

F E A D G C A B D E

G A F D B A C G A F

11 Write the indicated notes (use o). Make sure each note is legible. The first time G and A appear, write them in the low register, the second time in the high register.

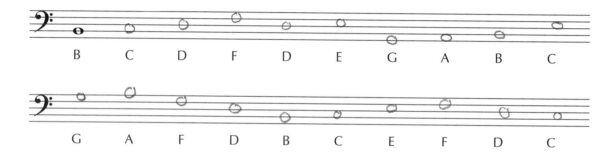

B C D F D E G A B C

G A F D B C E F D C

Ledger Lines

To notate pitches above or below the five-line staff, it is necessary to extend that staff by the addition of **ledger lines**. Notice that the alternation of line-and-space names continues:

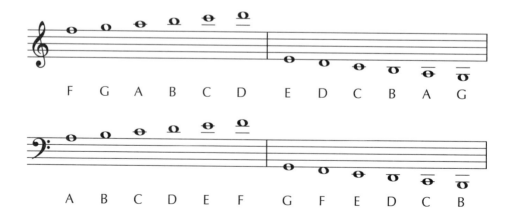

F G A B C D E D C B A G

A B C D E F G F E D C B

Ledger lines are not added above a note when it lies above the staff, or below a note when it lies below the staff:

correct   incorrect

Writing Ledger Lines

The space between a staff line and a ledger line or between ledger lines is the same as the space between staff lines:

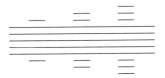

12 Copy each note. Be careful to space the ledger lines equidistantly. Make sure your notehead is legible. Name each note.

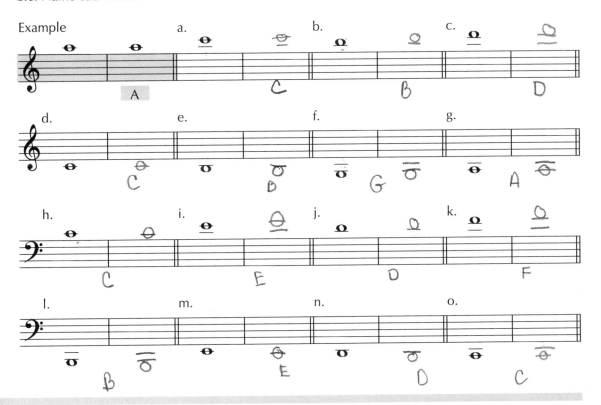

The Grand Staff

The treble and bass clefs are often joined to form the **grand staff**. Also called the **great staff** or **piano staff**, this familiar layout allows both high and low pitches to be presented simultaneously.

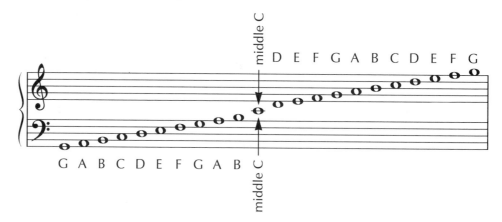

Middle C

The C midway on the piano keyboard lies exactly between the two staves. This C, called **middle C**, appears on the first ledger line below the treble clef and on the first ledger line above the bass clef. Written either way, middle C is the same note.

TWO SPELLINGS OF MIDDLE C

Learning Note Names

To read music, you must be able to recognize the notes in both clefs instantly. If you don't establish a secure basis in note reading now, further study will be difficult. The following exercises will help you develop this facility.

13   Rearrange these note patterns from lowest to highest. Name all notes. Notice that a different type of note (a quarter note) is being used. (See *Rhythm Reader*, Chapter One.)

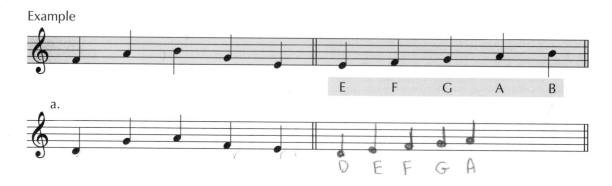

14 Rearrange the notes in order, from highest to lowest. Name all notes.

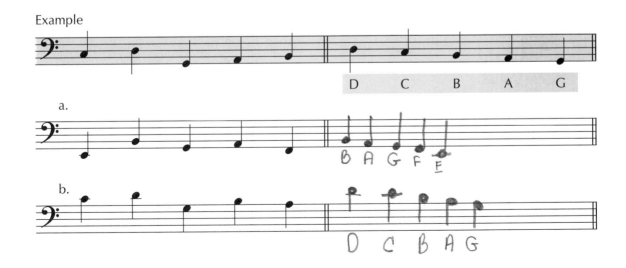

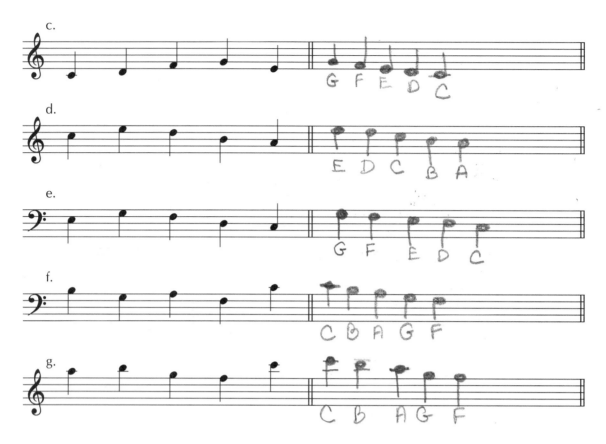

15 In the following exercises, write the given note in the bass clef if it is first presented in the treble clef; write the given note in the treble clef if it is presented in the bass clef. Be sure to include all clefs. Name each note. Study the example carefully.

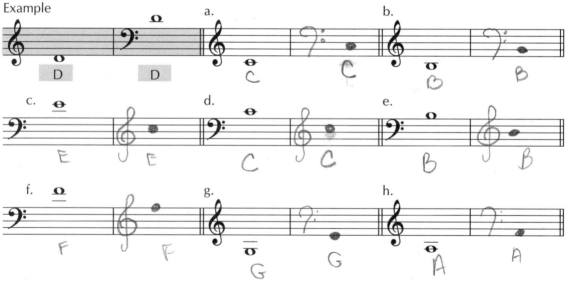

16 Look at the group of notes in the staff marked "Study" below. Memorize the position of each note. Then, keeping an even beat, name out loud each note in the staves marked "Speak." Do not write the note names. Record the time (in seconds) of your fastest accurate reading. There is space for future timings, so that you can come back to this exercise while studying later chapters.

a. Study:

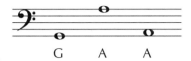

Speak:

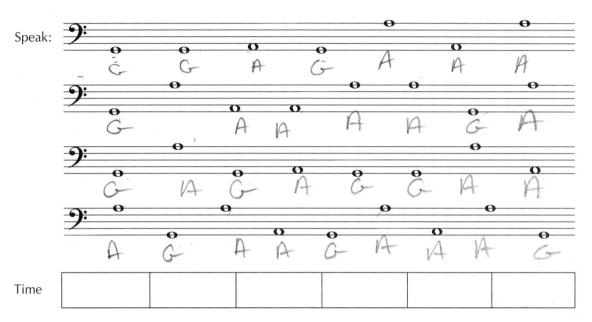

Time

b. Study:

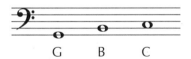

Speak:

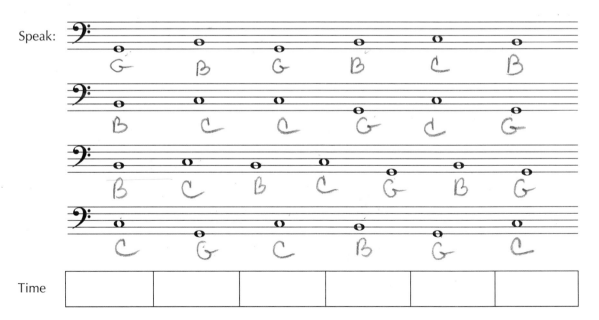

Time

c. Study:

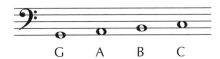

G   A   B   C

Speak:

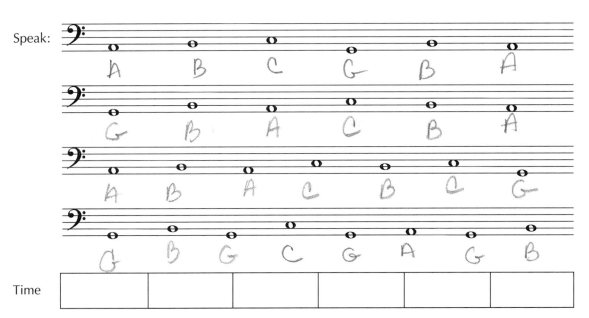

Time

d. Study:

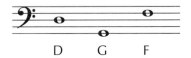

D   G   F

Speak:

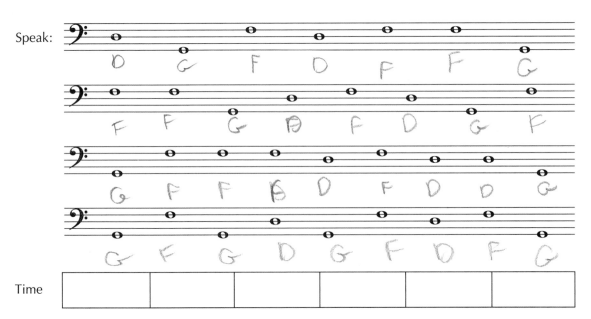

Time

e. Study:

A   G   E

Speak:

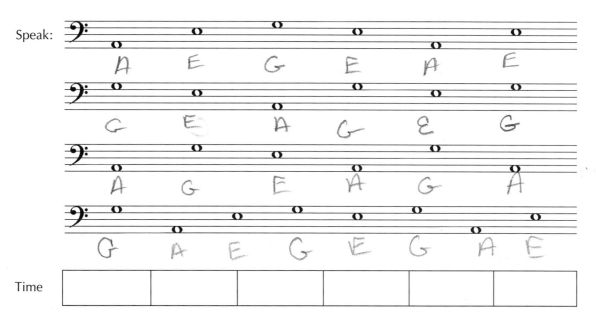

Time

f. Study:

G   F   G   A   B

Speak:

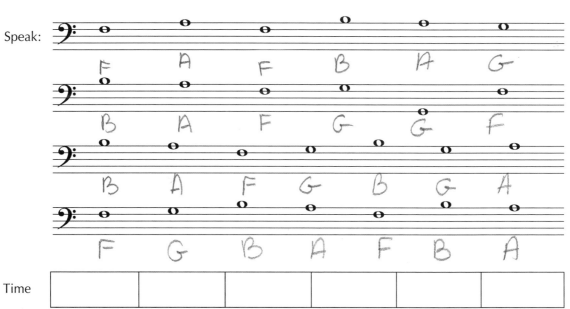

Time

g. Study:

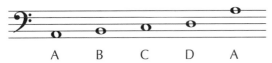

A   B   C   D   A

Speak:

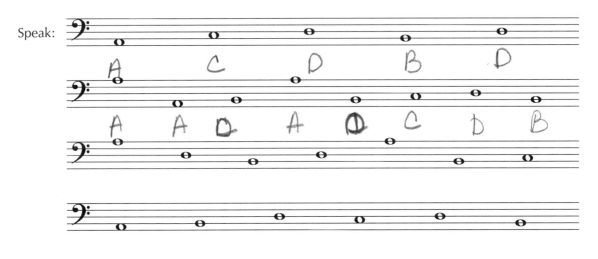

A   C   D   B   D

A   A   D   A   D   C   D   B

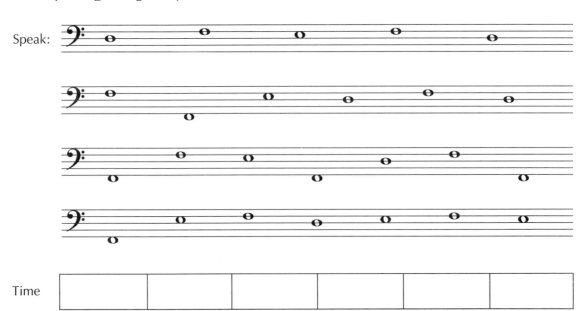

Time

h. Study:

F   D   E   F

Speak:

Time

17 Follow the same instructions as for #16.

a. Study:

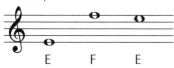

E   F   E

Speak:

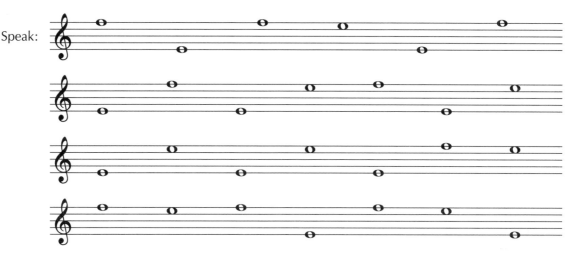

Time

b. Study:

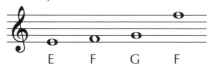

E   F   G   F

Speak:

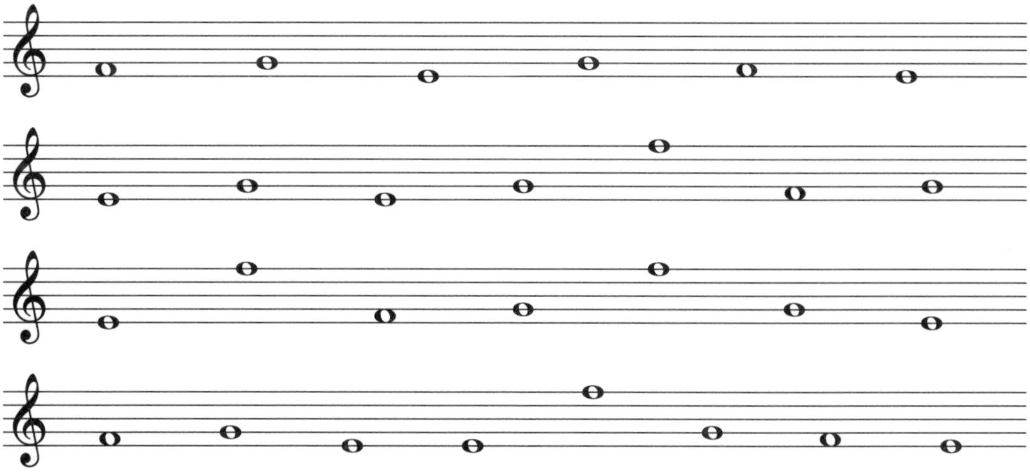

Time

c. Study:

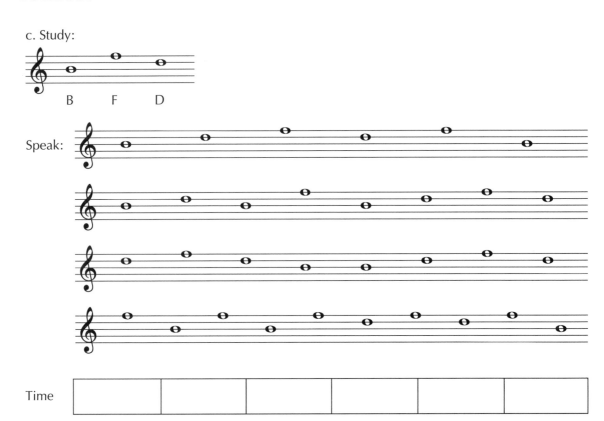

B   F   D

Speak:

Time						

d. Study:

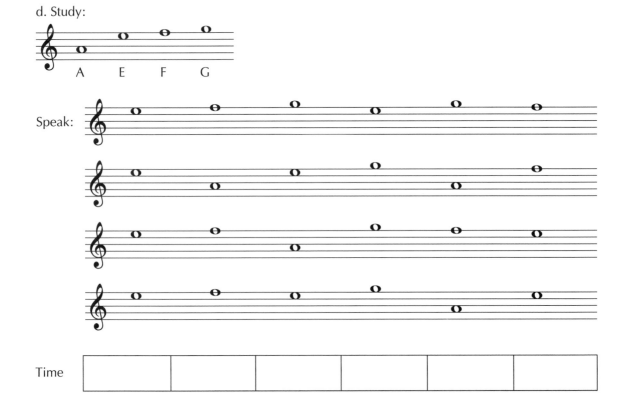

A   E   F   G

Speak:

Time						

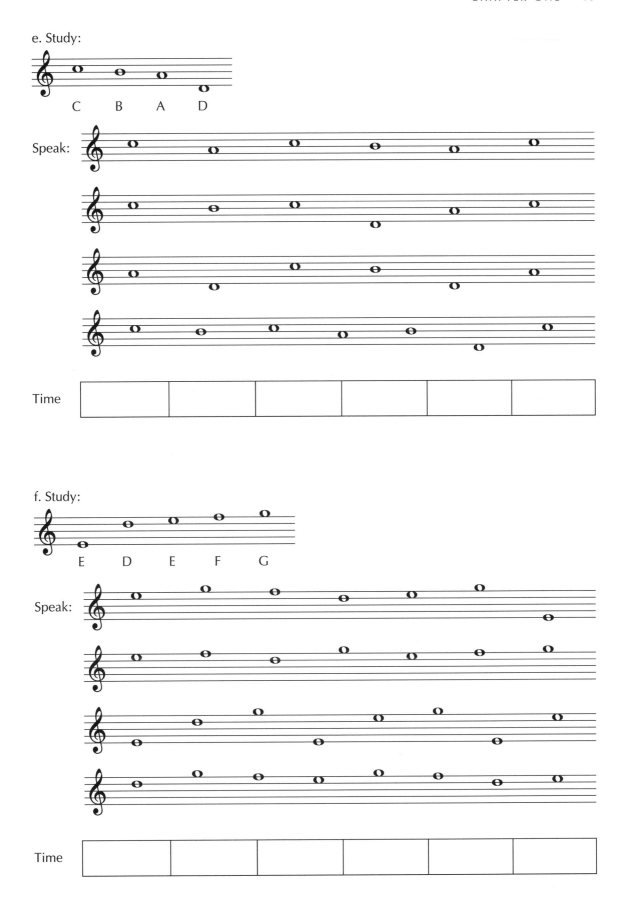

g. Study:

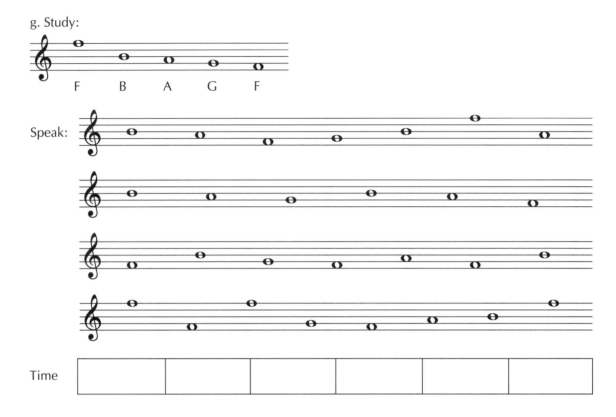

F   B   A   G   F

18   Name the following notes aloud, speaking at a moderate but steady pace. Review previous exercises as needed. Identifying these pitches quickly and accurately is an important goal for your work in this chapter. Record the time (in seconds) of your fastest accurate reading. Additional space has been provided for future timings.

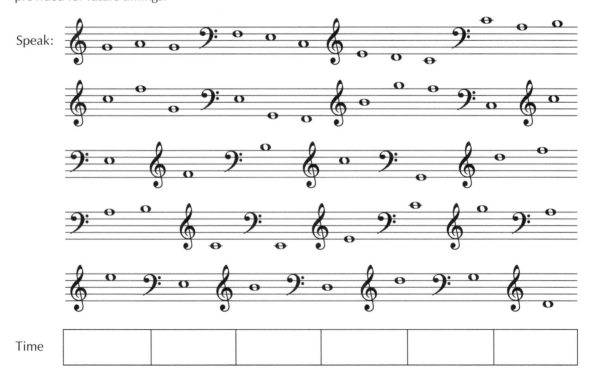

TERMS, SYMBOLS, AND CONCEPTS

Define the following terms, symbols, or concepts. Consult both the text and Glossary (see p. 254). If you use the definition found in the Glossary, you may wish to expand it by (1) restating it in your own words; (2) adding information from the text; or (3) providing an example. Use music manuscript paper as needed.

notation

note

pitch   ledger lines

staff   grand staff

octave*   middle C

register

SUGGESTED ACTIVITIES

1. Draw a treble clef on music manuscript paper. Starting two ledger lines below and ending two ledger lines above, write in and name all the notes from memory. Repeat the process in the bass clef.

2. Using a guitar or other stringed instrument, discover how pitch is affected by

   • shortening the string;
   • making the string looser;
   • tightening the string.

*Define this term without using the Glossary.

CHAPTER TWO

The Piano Keyboard

The piano is a basic instrument for the study of music, and a working knowledge of its keyboard is essential for musicianship. The arrangement of the piano keys *parallels the system of notation*. Throughout this book, you will find diagrams illustrating the relationship between the written note on the staff and its position on the keyboard. This relationship will help you understand not only notation but also many aspects of music theory. These diagrams, however, cannot replace playing or hearing music on a piano or other keyboard instrument.

Other Keyboards

There are many keyboard instruments besides the traditional piano: the electronic synthesizer, chromatic xylophone, and accordion are three examples of instruments with the same keyboard arrangement as the piano. When you are instructed in this book to play a simple melody or exercise on the keyboard, make an effort to do so! Performing simple melodies and exercises, even slowly, will greatly enhance your enjoyment and understanding of the material in this book.

The Design of the Keyboard

Look at the keyboard below. The first thing to notice is the way the black keys are grouped: alternating clusters of twos and threes. This pattern helps identify notes across the entire keyboard span.

The White Keys

The white keys are named from A to G, exactly like the lines and spaces on the staff. Take special notice of the C key.

C is always the white key to the left of each group of two black keys. It is often used as a point of reference for locating other keys.

1   a. Write the letter D on each D key:

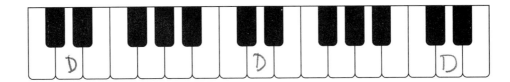

b. Write the letter E on each E key:

c. Write the letter F on each F key:

d. Write the letter G on each G key:

e. Write the letter A on each A key:

f. Write the letter B on each B key:

The Black Keys

Each black key lies halfway between two white keys. If you play a black key and its neighboring white keys, you will hear that the pitch of the black key is halfway between the two white keys. Each black key is named by referring to its position either above or below a neighboring white key.

NAMING BLACK KEYS

1. The black key immediately above (to the right of) the white key is named by adding a **sharp** (♯) to the white key name. A sharp (♯) is the musical symbol that indicates the note has been *raised* in pitch.
2. The black key immediately below (to the left of) a white key is named by adding a **flat** (♭) to the white key name. A flat (♭) is the musical symbol that indicates the note has been *lowered* in pitch.

Enharmonic Spelling

Each black key has *two* possible names, depending on the white key used to name it. For example, C♯ (pronounced "C sharp") can also be notated as D♭ (pronounced "D flat"). Notating the same pitch with a different name is called **enharmonic spelling**. As another example, an enharmonic spelling for F♯ is G♭. Both spellings indicate the same note:

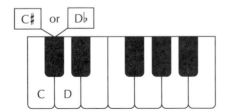 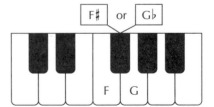

2 Name these notes in two ways, using ♯ and ♭ signs.

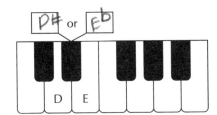

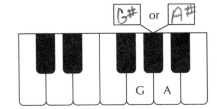

3 Fill in the black key that corresponds to the indicated note. Also write its enharmonic equivalent in the box provided. Study the example carefully.

Example:

G♭ (G flat) or F♯

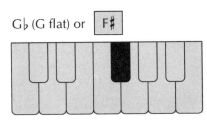

a. F♯ (F sharp) or G♭

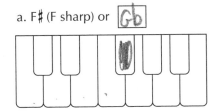

b. A♭ (A flat) or G♯

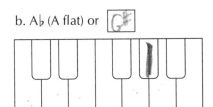

c. B♭ (B flat) or A♯

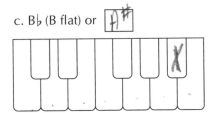

d. C♯ (C sharp) or D♭

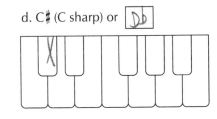

e. E♭ (E flat) or D♯

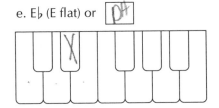

f. D♯ (D sharp) or E♭

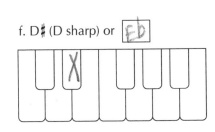

g. G♯ (G sharp) or [A♭]

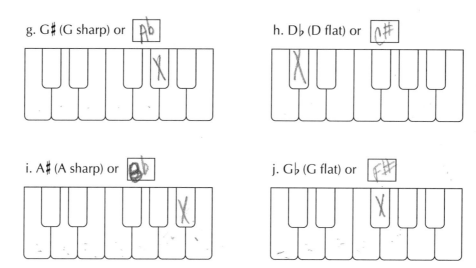

h. D♭ (D flat) or [C♯]

i. A♯ (A sharp) or [B♭]

j. G♭ (G flat) or [F♯]

4   Write and play all the keyboard notes within an octave starting and ending on C, first ascending with sharps, then descending with flats.

Ascending: C   C♯   D   D♯   E   F   F♯   G   G♯   A   A♯   B   C

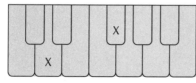

Descending: C   B   B♭   A   A♭   G   G♭   F   E   E♭   D   D♭   C

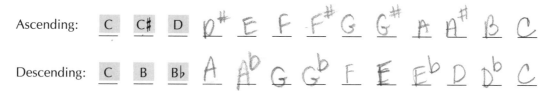

Practice saying these ascending and descending patterns from memory while imagining or playing them on the keyboard.

5   In the exercises below, mark each indicated key with an X. Study the example carefully.

Example:

D and F♯

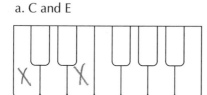

a. C and E

b. C♯ and A

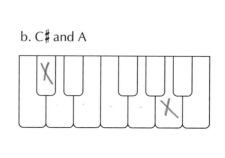

c. D♭ and A♯

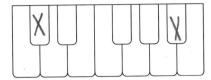

d. B♭ and E

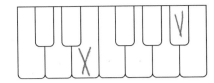

e. E♭ and B

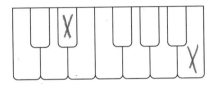

f. F♯ and G♯

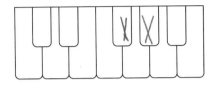

g. G♭ and A♭

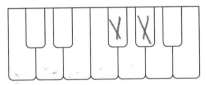

h. F♯ and F

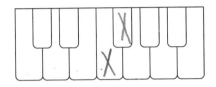

i. C and D♭

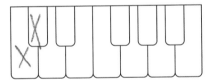

j. G and B♭

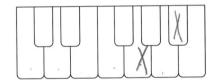

Notating the White Keys

The white keys are notated on successive lines and spaces in both keys. Study the relationship between the notes on the staff and their equivalents on the keyboard.

TREBLE CLEF

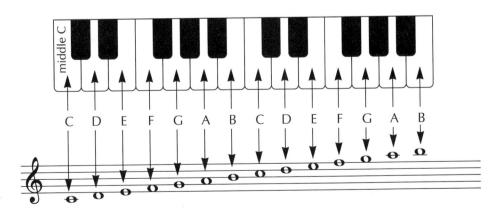

BASS CLEF

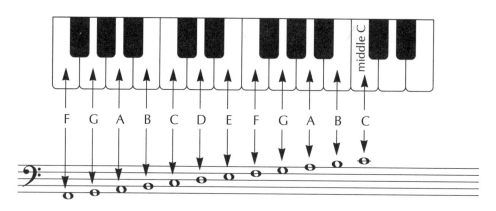

---

6 Name each note marked with an X on the keyboard. Then write the notes on the staff. Use the type of notehead indicated (o or ●).

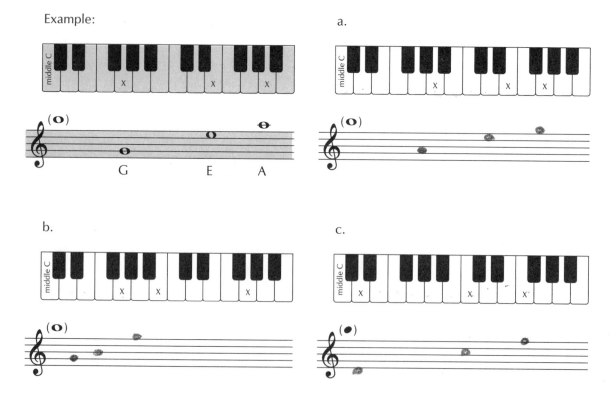

d.

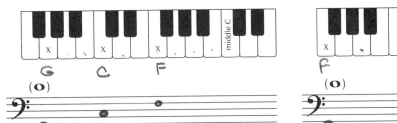

e.

7   Follow the same instructions as for #6.

a.

b.

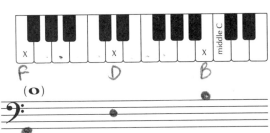

c.

d.

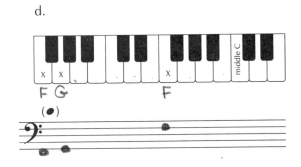

e.

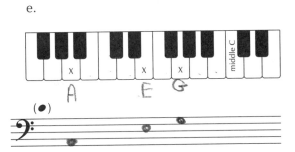

f.

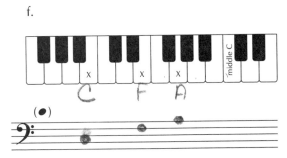

Notating the Black Keys

The black keys are notated on the staff by placing either a sharp or a flat before the notehead. For example:

A♯ is notated   D♭ is notated

Notice that the sharp or flat falls precisely on the same line or in the same space as the notehead.

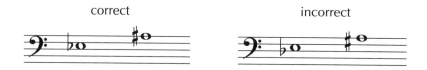

correct   incorrect

8 Practice writing sharps and flats in the spaces or around the lines, as indicated in the handwritten examples. Take care to write each sharp and flat legibly.

9 Write each of these notes marked with an X, first with a sharp and then with a flat (its enharmonic equivalent). Name each note.

Example:

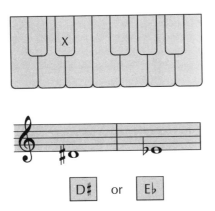

D♯ or E♭

a.

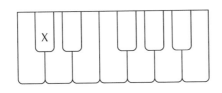

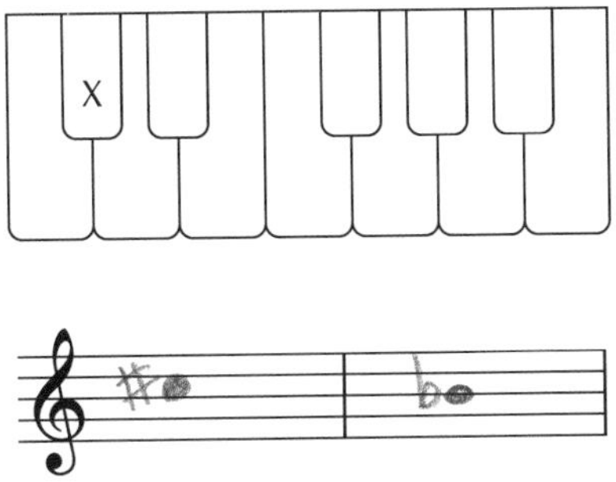

C♯ or B♭

b.

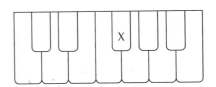

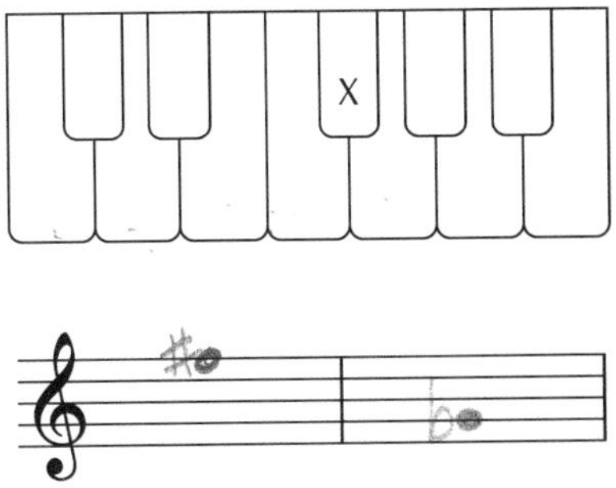

F♯ or G♭

c.

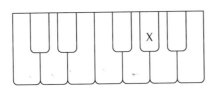

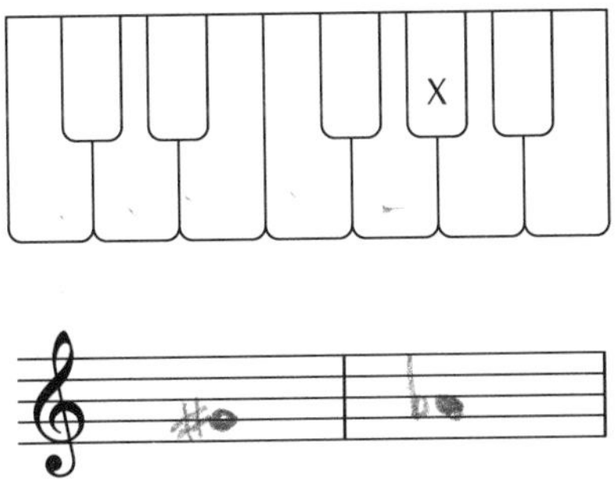

G♯ or A♭

d.

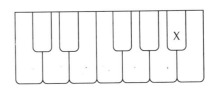

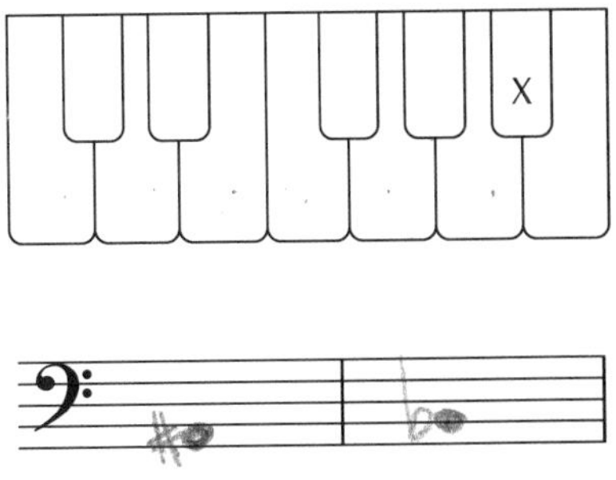

A♯ or B♭

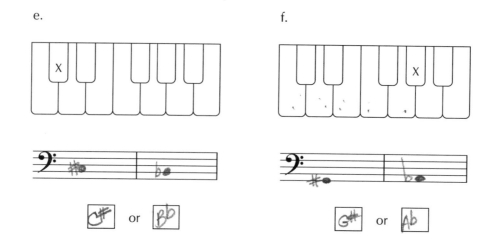

e.   f.

C♯ or B♭   G♯ or A♭

TERMS, SYMBOLS, AND CONCEPTS

keyboard plan (location of black   ♭
  and white keys)   enharmonic spelling
♯

SUGGESTED ACTIVITIES

1. Practice playing all the C's on the keyboard as fast as you can. When you can negotiate all the C's, proceed to each of the other keys.
2. Think of three different notes. Visualize their position on the keyboard, then play them.
3. Draw a keyboard from memory.
4. Using the keyboard from Activity 3, name all the notes ascending from C an octave up to the next C. Repeat this process descending.

CHAPTER THREE

Half Steps and Whole Steps

The previous chapters dealt with notation and its relationship to the keyboard. In this chapter, we will begin to explore two of the basic building blocks of musical structure. Knowledge of half steps and whole steps on both staff and keyboard is essential for understanding our musical tradition.

Half Steps

A **half step** is the smallest measurable distance in the traditional Western system of music. On the keyboard, a half step is the distance between two immediately adjacent keys. There are twelve half steps within an octave.

1 Play all the half steps within an octave from C to C.

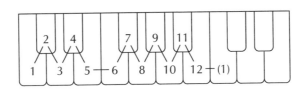

Notice that between white keys, half steps occur *only* in two places, E–F and B–C, because those are the only white keys that have no black key between them. Memorizing the location of these white-key half steps will greatly facilitate your understanding of musical notation.

2 Play E–F and B–C.

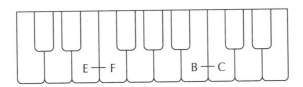

> **KEYBOARD HALF STEPS**
> 1. E–F and B–C are the only half steps on the white keys.
> 2. All other half steps occur between a black key and the nearest white key, or between a white key and the nearest black key.

3 Draw an arrow to the key one half step *above* each indicated note, as in the example.

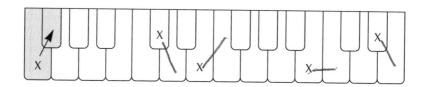

4 Draw an arrow to the key one half step *below* each indicated note, as in the example.

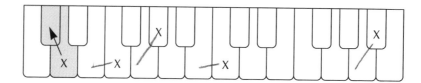

Whole Steps

A **whole step** consists of two half steps. Observe the following whole steps on the keyboard below. Notice the various places where whole steps occur: from white to white key, black to black key, white to black key, and black to white key.

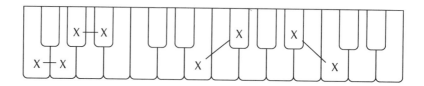

5   Draw an arrow to the key a whole step *above* the indicated note.

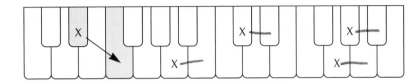

6   Draw an arrow to the key a whole step *below* the indicated note.

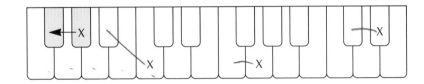

7   Answer the following questions.

a.   The half step is the ___Smallest___ distance we can measure on the keyboard.

b.   How many half steps make up a whole step? ___2___

c.   The distances between all the white keys on the keyboard are whole steps except the distances between ___F___ and ___G___.

Semitone and Whole Tone

In music theory, there is often more than one term for a specific concept. For example, different terms exist for the half step and whole step. The half step is also called a **semitone**, and the whole step is also called a **whole tone**. The terms are used interchangeably.

Semitone Types

There are two types of semitones (half steps), differentiated by how they are notated. One type uses the *same letter name* and falls on the same line or space on the staff:

F   F♯   B   B♭

The other type uses *two consecutive letter names* and falls a line or space away:

F♯   G   B   C

Observe that the same semitone can be notated in two ways:

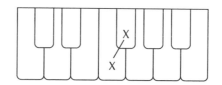

same   consecutive
letter name   letter names

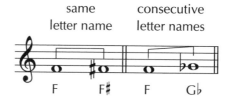

F   F♯   F   G♭

8   Notate each of the following keyboard half steps, as in the example. First use different letter names, then use the same letter name. Name each note.

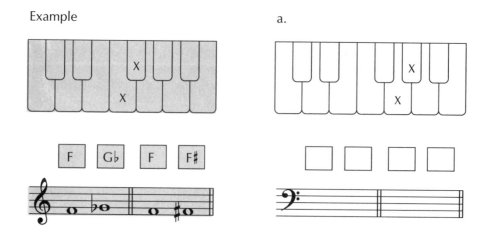

Example

a.

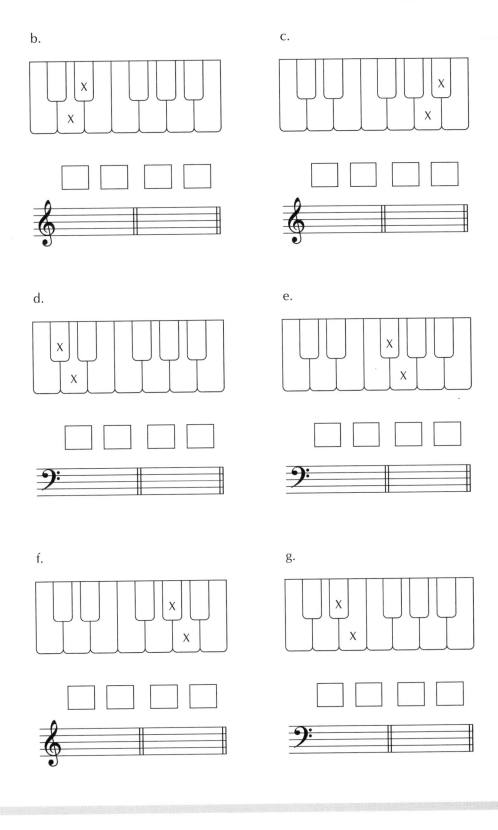

Accidentals

Symbols that alter the pitch of a note are called **accidentals**. We have used two so far: the sharp and the flat. Altogether, there are five accidentals. The following exercise presents their names, symbols, and functions.

9   Play.

a. The **sharp** (♯) *raises* the pitch of a note a half step (semitone):

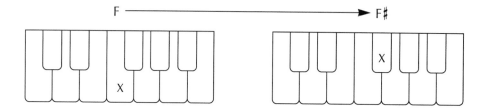

b. The **flat** (♭) *lowers* the pitch of a note a half step (semitone):

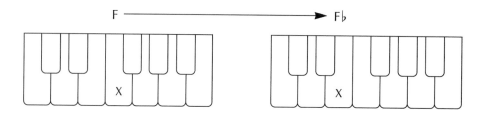

c. The **natural** (♮) *cancels* the accidental:

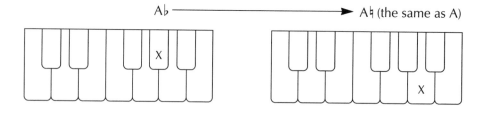

d. The **double sharp** (𝄪) *raises* the pitch one whole step (whole tone):

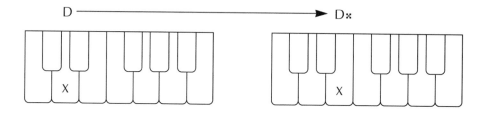

e. The **double flat** (♭♭) *lowers* the pitch one whole step (whole tone):

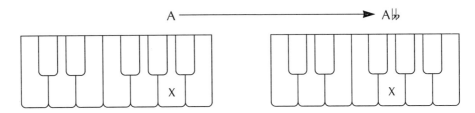

A ⟶ A♭♭

It is important to be aware that a note with an accidental is not always a black key, but can be a white key. Accidentals are indications of a function—the alteration of a pitch.

SUMMARY OF ACCIDENTALS

1. A sharp (♯) raises the pitch of a note a half step.
2. A flat (♭) lowers the pitch of a note a half step.
3. A natural (♮) cancels a previous accidental.
4. A double sharp (𝄪) raises the pitch of a note a whole step.
5. A double flat (♭♭) lowers the pitch of a note a whole step.

---

10 Mark the key indicated by the accidental, as in the example. If in doubt, refer to the *function* of the accidental as given in the "Summary of Accidentals" box above.

Example:

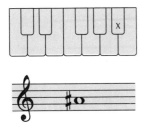

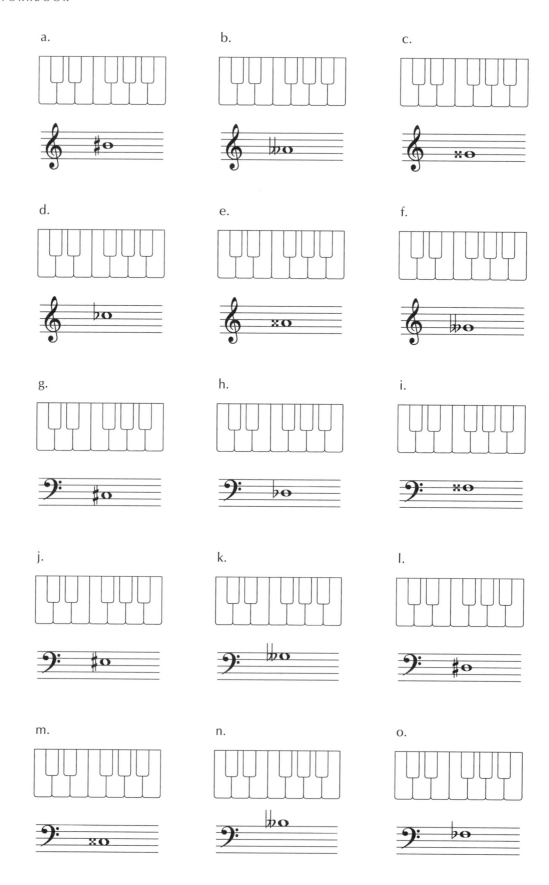

Accidentals in a Measure

Once an accidental has altered the pitch of a note, the note will remain altered for the duration of the measure in which it occurs. For example:

is played

However, an accidental in one measure does *not* affect the same note in the next measure:

is played

Nor does it affect the same note in a different octave:

is played

Use of the Natural

To cancel a sharp or flat, a natural sign is used. Once a natural sign is used on a note, it remains in effect for the *rest of the measure*. For example:

is played

Precautionary Accidentals

The natural sign may be used to identify any note whose pitch is in doubt because of a previous accidental. This practice is left to the discretion of the composer. These natural signs often appear in parentheses. For example, in the following excerpt from a Brahms piano accompaniment, notice the precautionary naturals on D and C in the second measure.

Brahms

11   Change each pitch by adding a natural. Indicate whether the addition of a natural raises or lowers the pitch by writing either "up ¹/₂ step" or "down ¹/₂ step" in the box provided below the staff. Name each pitch in the boxes above the staff. Use the keyboard as a reference. Study the examples carefully.

Examples:

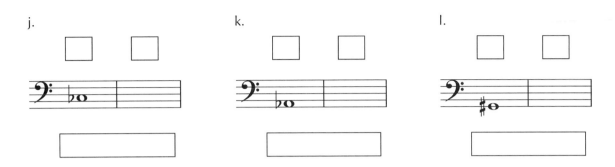

12 Write a note one whole step above or below the given pitch as indicated. Use the keyboard as a reference.

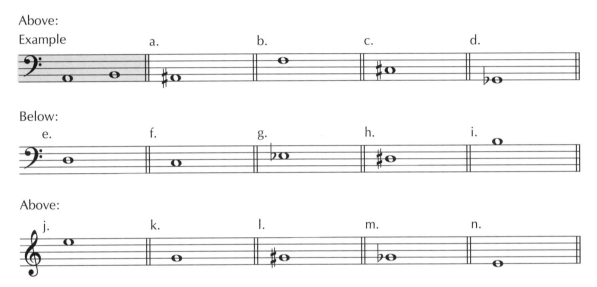

13 Write *two* enharmonic equivalents of each pitch (see p. 24). All accidentals may be used. Use the keyboard as reference.

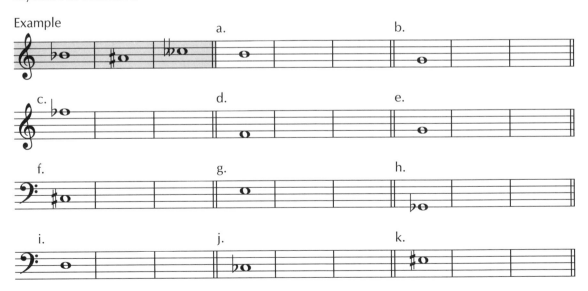

Visualizing a Keyboard

A skill that can help you in a variety of theoretical situations is the ability to visualize a keyboard. Think of its construction, especially the pattern of black keys and the two semitones that occur between white keys. Practice "seeing" a keyboard with your eyes closed until you actually can. Another way to visualize a keyboard is to actually draw a model of it from memory.

14 Instead of looking at a staff or keyboard, visualize it. Now answer the following questions:

a. What accidental would raise A a half step? _____

b. What accidental would raise D♭ a half step? _____

c. What accidental would lower G a half step? _____

d. What accidental would lower C♯ a half step? _____

e. What accidental would raise A a whole step? _____

f. What accidental would lower A a whole step? _____

g. Why don't you need an accidental to create a semitone above E? _____

_____

h. Is C♭ a white or a black key? _____

i. Name an enharmonic equivalent to E using a flat sign: _____

j. Name an enharmonic equivalent to C using a sharp sign: _____

TERMS, SYMBOLS, AND CONCEPTS

half step*	♭
whole step*	♮
semitone*	𝄪
whole tone*	♭♭
accidental	precautionary accidental
♯	

SUGGESTED ACTIVITIES

1. Listen to half steps and whole steps by playing them on the keyboard.
2. Draw a model of the keyboard from memory, and bracket all half steps on the white keys.
3. Using the keyboard from Activity 2, bracket a whole step on black keys, a whole step from a black key to a white key, and a whole step from a white key to a black key.

*Define without using the Glossary.

CHAPTER FOUR

Scales

In Italian, *scale* means ladder. Imagine for a moment that the rungs of a ladder are musical pitches. The result is a musical scale: a series of ascending or descending pitches. On a ladder, the distance between two adjacent rungs is a step; in a scale, the distance between two adjacent pitches is also a step.

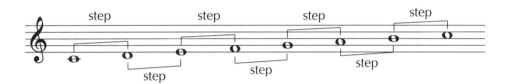

There are many kinds of scales, which differ in the size, number, and arrangement of the steps they contain.

Diatonic Scales

The term **diatonic scale** identifies a scale that uses *successive letter names* and contains five whole steps and two half steps. This scale is made up of seven different pitches, with the original pitch then repeated at the octave. The notes of the diatonic scale are referred to as **scale degrees**. The first and lowest scale degree is usually designated as number 1. The letter name of this first note gives the scale its name. The successive scale degrees are numbered 2, 3, 4, 5, 6, and 7; 8 has the same letter name as 1 but sounds an octave higher. There are various types of diatonic scales, depending on the position of the whole steps and half steps.

1 Write the notes and letter names of the following diatonic scales in ascending order. Do not use sharps or flats. Take care to use successive letter names. Each scale is of a different type (we will consider these types in Chapter Twelve), but all are diatonic. Study the example carefully.

Example:

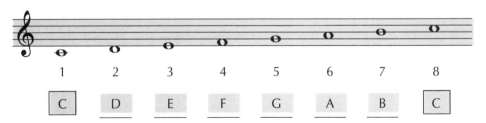

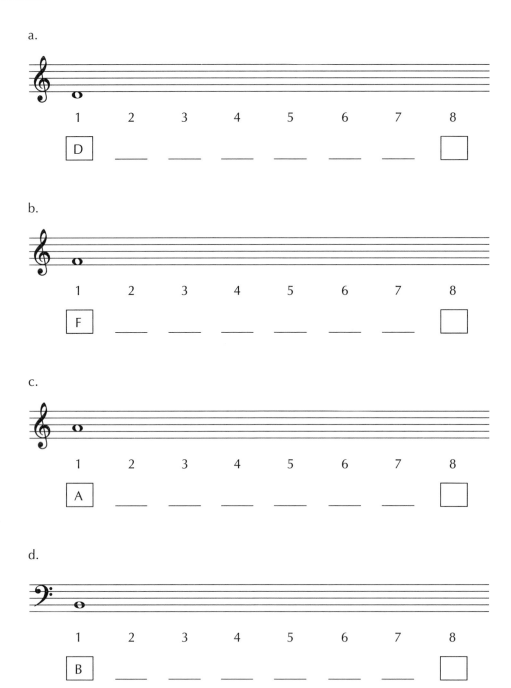

The Major Scale   The first diatonic scale we will study is the **major scale**. Its characteristic sound can be heard in *I Know Where I'm Going* (Cassette). The major scale is distinguished from other diatonic scales by the position of its five whole steps and two half steps. In the following major scale, beginning on C, the wholes steps are labeled "1," and the half steps are labeled "¹/₂."

C-Major Scale on the Keyboard

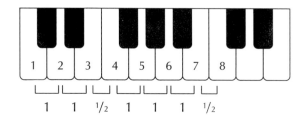

Notice the different ways in which numbers are used in the diagrams below: 1 through 8 identify scale degrees; 1 and ½ designate whole steps and half steps.

C-Major Scale on the Staff

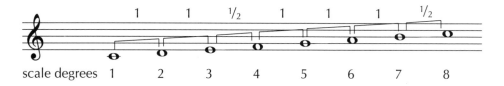

scale degrees   1   2   3   4   5   6   7   8

2 Complete the following statements about the major scale. Refer to the diagrams above.

a. Between scale degrees 1 and 2 is a _____ step.

b. Between scale degrees 2 and 3 is a _____ step.

c. Between scale degrees 3 and 4 is a _____ step.

d. Between scale degrees 4 and 5 is a _____ step.

e. Between scale degrees 5 and 6 is a _____ step.

f. Between scale degrees 6 and 7 is a _____ step.

g. Between scale degrees 7 and 8 is a _____ step.

MAJOR-SCALE PATTERN

All major scales have half steps between scale degrees 3 and 4 and between 7 and 8. All other steps are whole steps.

Building a Major Scale on D

Our objective now is to construct a major scale on D. But first let us examine why a diatonic scale on D without accidentals is not major. Study the scale below. Notice that it is a diatonic scale *because* it is spelled with consecutive letter names and has five whole steps and two half steps. It is *not* a major scale, however, because the whole steps and half steps are in the wrong places.

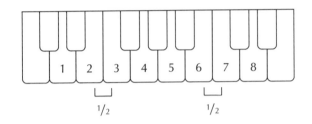

Play:

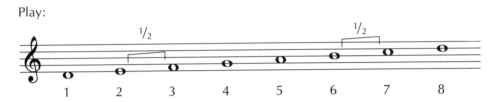

3   Complete the following sentences. Refer to the scale and diagram above.

a. The scale on D shown above is a diatonic scale because it is spelled with _____

_____.

b. This scale is not a major scale because the half steps occur between _____ and

_____ and between _____ and _____.

c. In a major scale, the half steps occur between _____ and _____ and between

_____ and _____.

Adding Accidentals to Form a Major Scale

To build a major scale on a pitch other than C, we must use accidentals (unless we use key signatures, discussed in Chapter Five). Since we need a whole step between scale degrees 2 and 3, we must raise F to F♯. This procedure also produces the required half step between scale degrees 3 and 4. Similarly, by raising C to C♯, we make a whole step between scale degrees 6 and 7 and a half step between 7 and 8. We have now formed a D-major scale, as illustrated on the keyboard and staff below.

MAJOR SCALE ON D

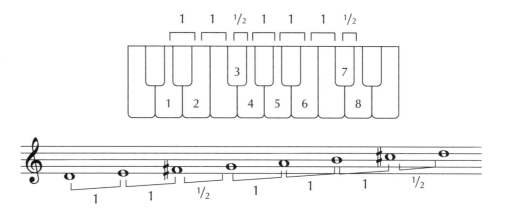

The Importance of Correct Spelling

Spelling a major scale correctly is important, as can be illustrated by the following enharmonic equivalent of a D-major scale:

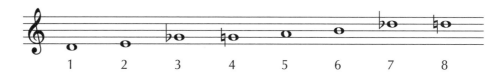

Although this pattern of pitches sounds the same as the correct D-major scale given just above, it does not look like a diatonic scale. The letter names are not all consecutive (for example, there are two Gs in a row). A properly spelled diatonic scale accurately represents the *steps* of a scale and is therefore easy to read.

4   Answer the following questions.

a. Is a major scale diatonic? _____

b. Are all diatonic scales major scales? _____

c. To build a major scale on a pitch other than C, you must add _____.

d. The enharmonically spelled scale on D shown immediately above is incorrect because

_____

_____

_____.

Major-Scale Spellings

Follow these steps for spelling major scales.

1. Start with the note that has the same name as the scale you are going to build. Then go up the staff with consecutive letter names until you reach the same note an octave above. You should now have eight notes.
2. If the scale starts on a note with an accidental, place the sharp or flat *immediately* before scale degrees 1 and 8.
3. Now add accidentals to form the correct whole-step/half-step pattern of the major scale. Scales with sharps do not use flats; scales with flats do not use sharps.

EXAMPLE: HOW TO CONSTRUCT THE E♭-MAJOR SCALE

Step 1

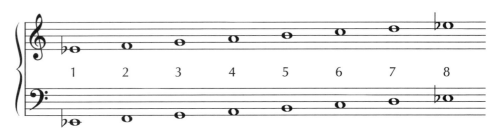

Step 2

Step 3

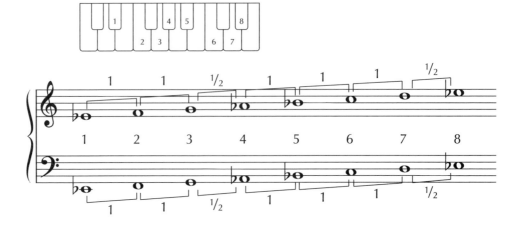

5 Write each indicated scale in both treble and bass clefs. Draw the appropriate clef on each staff first. Mark the scale steps on the keyboard.

Example: E major

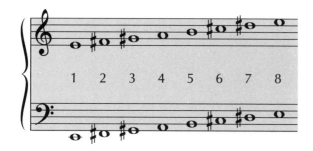

a. B♭ major

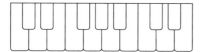

b. A major

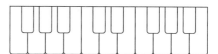

c. D major

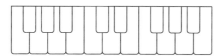

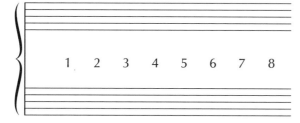

d. E major

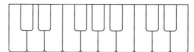

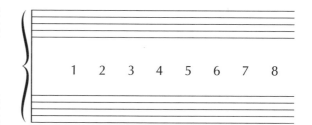

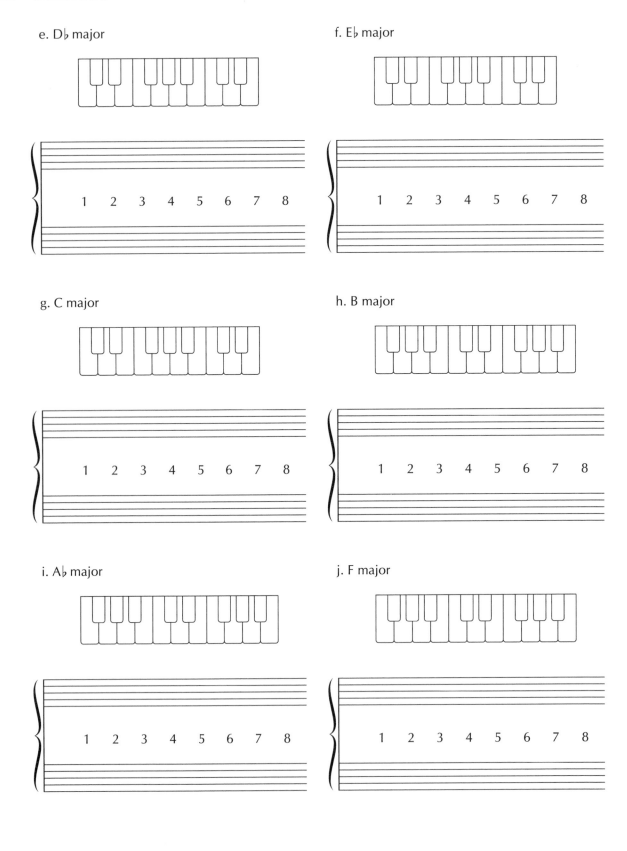

k. G major   l. F♯ major

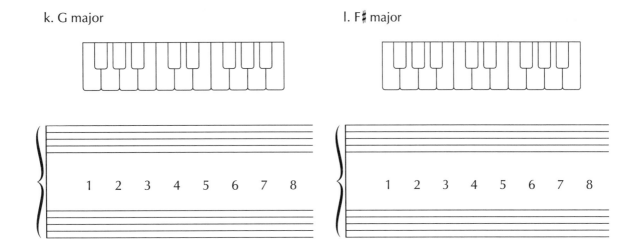

"In the Key of"   Music based on a scale built on a particular note is said to be "in the key of" that note. It may be further identified by a word indicating the type of scale. For example, a melody using pitches primarily from the major scale starting on D is said to be in the key of D major. (This concept will be explained more fully in Chapters Five and Six.)

Tonality   One of the defining aspects of most Western music, including classical music, popular music, and jazz, is **tonality**. This term refers to the fact that all of the pitches used in a piece (or section of a piece) relate to one central note, called the **tonic**. The tonic is the most prominent pitch, the pitch to which all others are drawn. We can therefore characterize the tonic as the "home" pitch, because it sounds prominent and stable in comparison with the other pitches. In a major scale, the tonic is the first degree of the scale. Thus, music in the key of E♭ major not only is based on the E♭-major scale but also has E♭ as its tonic pitch.

When we listen to the major scale, first ascending and then descending, we hear how the other scale degrees move away from and then back to the tonic. Music based on the system of tonality is called **tonal** music. We will learn much more about tonality in later chapters. Here, let us concentrate on its two main characteristics: (1) the relationship of various scale degrees to each other and (2) the pitch on which all scale degrees focus—the tonic.

6 Play (or have your instructor play) the following excerpts. Determine which note is the tonic. To make this decision, consider the following: (1) Which note sounds the most prominent? (2) To which major scale do the notes belong?

a.   Handel

tonic ☐

b.   Hymn tune

tonic ☐

c.   French-Canadian folk song

tonic ☐

d.   German folk melody

tonic ☐

e.   Mozart

tonic ☐

Melody

You have just listened to some **melodies**. Most likely you have been singing melodies all your life. One of the most important elements of music, melody is *musical action in time*, the combination of rhythm and a series of pitches in a unified flow. There are many types of melodies and many different ways of getting to know them. The *Scorebook* demonstrates this variety. As you explore these melodies, sometimes returning to the same melody several times, your knowledge of musical theory and structure will grow.

7 Sing the opening of a song you know. Repeat, tapping a pencil with each word or note. Repeat once again, but this time just tap, don't sing. You have now isolated the rhythmic component to the melody by tapping out the rhythm "in time." Now repeat this process with other songs you know.

Intervals

As we just saw, one way to tell the difference between melodies is to distinguish their different rhythmic patterns. Another way is to compare the particular pattern of pitches each melody contains. But before we can do this, we need to examine how the pitches that make up a melody relate to each other. The distance between any two pitches is called an **interval**. There are several different ways to measure this distance. In this chapter, we will start with the most basic method: counting the number of staff steps from one note to another. For example, the interval from F to B contains four staff steps (counting both the first and last notes):

Because of the four staff steps, the interval F to B is called a 4th. Observe this procedure in the following intervals:

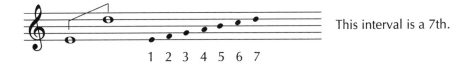

This interval is a 7th.

Notice that the number of staff steps includes both notes of the interval.

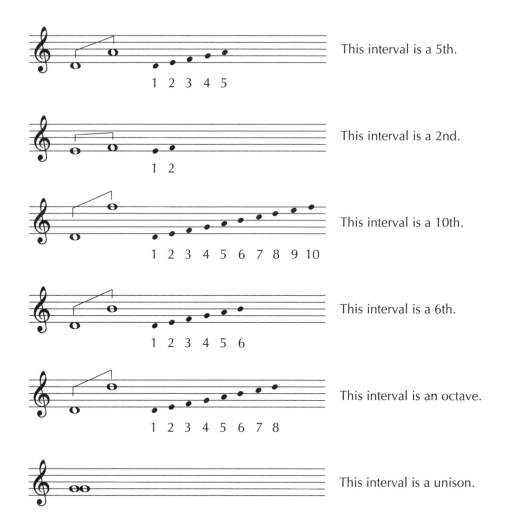

This interval is a 5th.

This interval is a 2nd.

This interval is a 10th.

This interval is a 6th.

This interval is an octave.

This interval is a unison.

8 Examine the following intervals. Write in the staff steps, but do not rewrite the original pitches of the interval. Number them and name the interval, as in the examples.

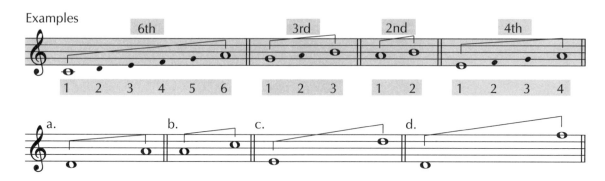

Melodic and Harmonic Intervals

In music, the two pitches of any interval occur in two ways: (1) one sounding after the other, thus forming a **melodic interval** and (2) both sounding at the same time, thus forming a **harmonic interval**. Both types of intervals are found in the next exercise.

9 Identify the following intervals by counting the staff steps. Do not notate the staff steps. Indicate which intervals are melodic and which are harmonic with an M or an H below the staff.

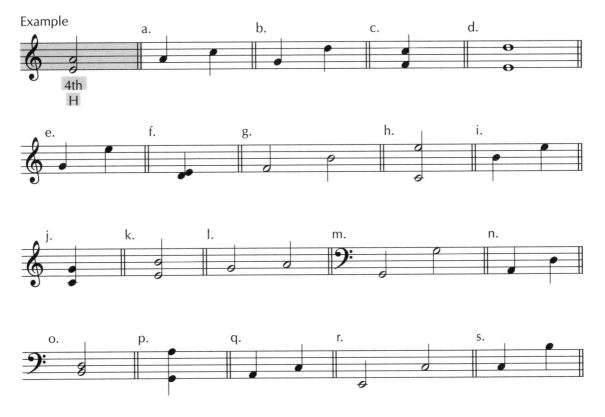

10 *Above* the given note, write the note that completes the correct harmonic interval. Observe the changes in clef signs, which remain in effect for the rest of that staff line.

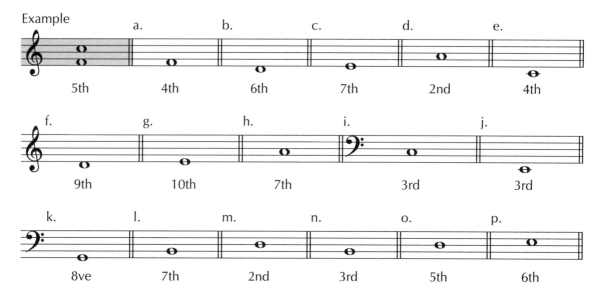

11 *Below* the given note, write the note that completes the correct melodic interval. Observe the changes in clef signs.

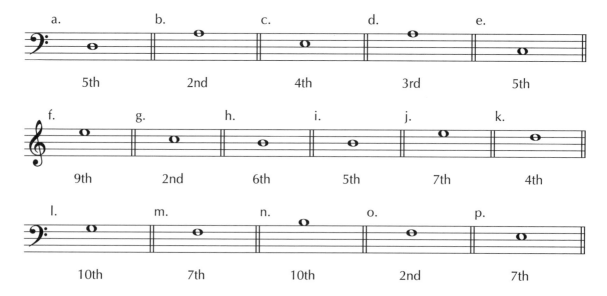

Melody and Intervals

A melody proceeds from one note to the next as a series of intervals. The number and order of these intervals is an important aspect of melodic design. One of the most common types of melodic movement is by 2nds. Because the 2nd makes up the steps of a scale, we describe a melody that moves by 2nds as **stepwise**, or say that it proceeds **by step**. When intervals of a 3rd occur, the melody is said to proceed by **skips**. Melodies with intervals larger than a 3rd are said to proceed by **leaps**.

stepwise melodic movement

melodic movement by skips

melodic movement by leaps

Few melodies lend themselves completely to one of these three classifications. Most often, melodies use all kinds of intervallic movement, usually in combination. Each type of melodic movement is bracketed in the following example:

Chorale Melody   J. S. Bach

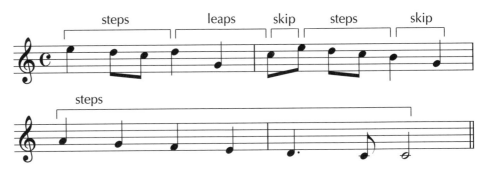

12   a. Examine the following melodies in the *Scorebook*. In the blanks below, write one of the following descriptions: *mostly stepwise* or *mostly skips and leaps*. Mostly stepwise doesn't mean you won't find some skips and leaps, and mostly skips and leaps doesn't mean you won't find some stepwise movement. What concerns us here is which type predominates in each melody.

Mozart, *Minuet* (*Scorebook* 73) _____

Oliver and the Maiden (*Scorebook* 7) _____

Brochan Lom (*Scorebook* 6) _____

Beethoven, *Ode to Joy* (*Scorebook* 59) _____

   b. Examine Morley's *Nancie* (*Scorebook* 61). Bracket and label one instance each of stepwise movement, movement by skip, and movement by leap.

   c. In *Nancie*, find the largest leap in the melody. What interval is it? _____

   d. Look at the theme from Mozart's *Symphony No. 29* (*Scorebook* 69). The melody alternates

between _____ and _____.

Inversion

When the lower note of an interval is replaced by the same note an octave higher, or when the higher note is replaced by the same note an octave lower, the interval is **inverted**. For example:

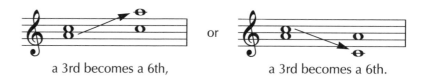

a 3rd becomes a 6th,   or   a 3rd becomes a 6th.

In the examples above, a 3rd is inverted both up and down. The inversion of a 3rd (in either direction) is a 6th.

There is a numerical relationship between the original interval and its inversion: when you add the numbers of the intervals together, you always get the number 9. Another way of stating this relationship is: to find the number of an inverted interval, subtract the number of the original interval from 9. For example, what is the inversion of a 4th? Subtract 4 from 9; the inversion of a 4th is a 5th. Remember, however, that when you add the intervals of a 4th and 5th, you get an octave (8ve), not a 9th.

13 Invert each of the following intervals two ways. FIrst shift the lower note of the original interval up an octave. Then shift the higher note down an octave. Name all intervals.

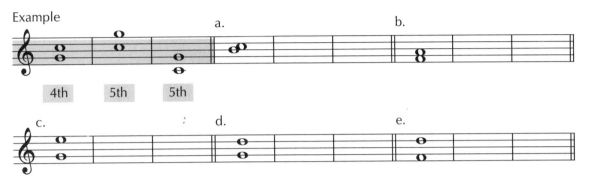

14 Complete the following statements about intervals.

a. An interval is measured by the number of _____ it contains.

b. Intervals with notes that sound together are called _____.

c. Intervals with notes that sound one after the other are called _____.

d. When the lower or higher note of an interval is switched an octave, the interval has been

_____.

e. The inversion of a 5th is a _____.

f. The inversion of a 2nd is a _____.

g. The inversion of a 6th is a _____.

TERMS, SYMBOLS, AND CONCEPTS

diatonic scales

scale degrees

constructing a major scale

"in the key of"

tonality

tonic

melody

interval

melodic interval

harmonic interval

melodic movement by step

melodic movement by skip

melodic movement by leap

inversion

SUGGESTED ACTIVITIES

1. Visualize a keyboard, and construct major scales without looking at an actual keyboard or staff.

2. Examine the following melodies for type of melodic movement (step, skip, and leap).

   Mozart, Theme from *Don Giovanni* (*Scorebook* 60)

   Group Song (*Scorebook* 2)

   Lullaby (Apache) (*Scorebook* 1)

3. Compose a short melody of at least eight measures, using rhythms that you know, and featuring various types of melodic movement.

CHAPTER FIVE

Key Signatures

A melody retains its identity in any major key because the relationship between the scale degrees is constant. We have found, however, that major scales can *look quite different* depending on what note the scale begins on (see pp. 51–53). For example, a major scale that begins on C uses no accidentals, a major scale that begins on A♭ requires four flats, a major scale on D calls for two sharps, and so forth. A system of **key signatures** organizes the use of accidentals in tonal music. Before mastering key signatures, we will work through several music examples that demonstrate how key signatures simplify musical notation.

1 Play and observe the following melodic opening, which is given in three different keys. Take special notice that the same pattern of scale steps is repeated in each version.

a. Using the scale of C major (in the key of C major):

American Folk Tune

1 3 5 5   2 3 4   1 3 5 5   2 3 2

b. Using the scale of D major (in the key of D major):

1 3 5 5   2 3 4   1 3 5 5   2 3 2

c. Using the scale of A♭ major (in the key of A♭ major):

1 3 5 5   2 3 4   1 3 5 5   2 3 2

We encounter two difficulties when we write this melody in different keys:

(1) We need to keep repeating the necessary accidentals throughout the opening of this tune.
(2) The same pattern of scale steps *looks different* in different keys, although we know it sounds the same.

**Adding a
Key Signature**

Let us now consider another melodic excerpt without a key signature. Notice the melodic pattern of steps and skips.

Key of D major

In Chapter Four, we discovered that the key of D major needs F♯ and C♯. In the example below, note how the key signature, which always appears at the beginning of the staff line, simplifies the notation by eliminating the need to write each accidental as it occurs. Notice the two accidentals that comprise the key signature. They are F♯ and C♯. Once these sharps are written *in the key signature*, all subsequent Fs and Cs become F♯s and C♯s *in all octaves*. Play this example, remembering that you are playing exactly the same melody that is notated above.

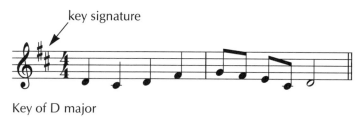

Key of D major

2   Now play a pattern of steps and skips that starts on B♭.

a. Key of B♭ major (without a key signature):

b. Key of B♭ major (with a key signature):

3   Now compare the following melodies, notated with key signatures, with the versions of these melodies shown in exercise #1, notated without them.

a. Key of C major

b. Key of D major

c. Key of A♭ major

Looking at these examples, we see that key signatures have solved the two problems of notating the same melodic pattern in different keys:

(1) There is no need to write the accidentals continually.
(2) The same musical pattern of intervals looks the same in each key.

4 In each of the following melodies, circle all notes altered by the key signature. Notice that sharps and flats affect their own letter name *in any octave*. Study the example carefully before proceeding.

Example

a.

b.

c.

d.

e.

f.

5 In the following exercises, write the actual note name resulting from the use of the key signature. Also, mark its position on the keyboard. Remember, the key signature applies to *all* octaves.

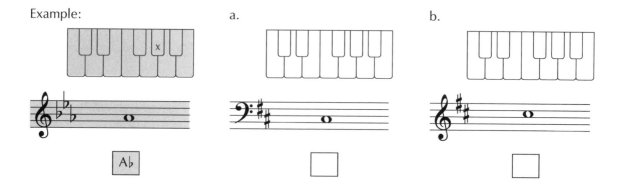

Example: a. b.

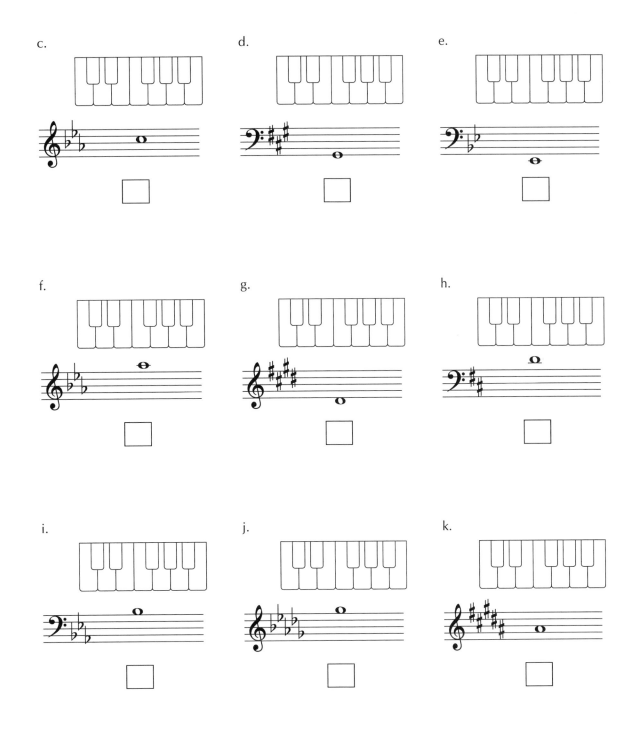

Organization of Major-Scale Key Signatures

The fifteen major-scale key signatures are organized in the following manner. Study the arrangement and order of sharps and flats.

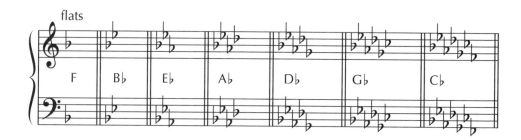

The sharps and flats of the key signatures reveal a pattern of intervals based on 5ths and 4ths. Look at the key signatures above. The one for G major has one sharp: F♯. The key signature for D major, with two sharps, shares the same F♯ but adds a C♯, a 4th below F♯ on the staff. The next key signature, for A major, requires the addition of G♯, a 5th above C♯. The pattern continues down a 4th for E major, adding a D♯ below G♯.

Thus, to form the correct pattern when building key signatures for sharp keys, go down a 4th, up a 5th, down a 4th, up a 5th, and so forth. The only exception to this rule is when adding the fifth sharp, A♯, for the key of B major; the A♯ is obtained by going a 4th below the D♯ that precedes it rather than going a 5th above. But remember from Chapter Four that *the inversion of a 5th is a 4th.* Therefore, moving down a 4th identifies the *same letter name* as moving up a 5th. The pattern then continues its regularity for the last two keys, F♯ and C♯, to complete the signatures for all seven sharp keys.

The sequence of flats for the flat keys follows a mirror image of the same pattern: up a 4th, down a 5th, up a 4th, down a 5th, and so forth, without exception. F major starts with one accidental, B♭. The next key, B♭, requires the addition of E♭, written a 4th above. Then down a 5th for the three flats of E♭ major, and so on through all seven flat keys.

The Circle of 5ths   The patterns of the sharp and flat key signatures can best be exemplified by a well-known diagram called the **circle of 5ths**. This diagram presents the order of keys and the number of accidentals for each key in a logical way, starting from the key of C major at the top of the circle. Note that when moving clockwise around the circle, the order of sharp keys unfolds, and when moving counterclockwise from C major, the order of flat keys unfolds.

The circle of 5ths derives its name from the fact that each key, when traveling around the circle, is a 5th away from the preceding one. For instance, when moving clockwise from C major, the key of G major is a 5th away (going *upward* on the staff) and has one sharp; the key of D major is a 5th away from G major and contains two sharps, and so forth. Similarly, when moving counterclockwise from C major, the key of F major, with one flat, is a 5th away (going *downward* on the staff); the key of B♭ major, with two flats, is a 5th away from F major, and so on.

Notice that at the bottom of the circle, three keys overlap. The overlapping keys—B and C♭, F♯ and G♭, and C♯ and D♭—are enharmonic versions of each other. While each pair is played on exactly the same keys on the piano, they are notated completely differently on the staff.

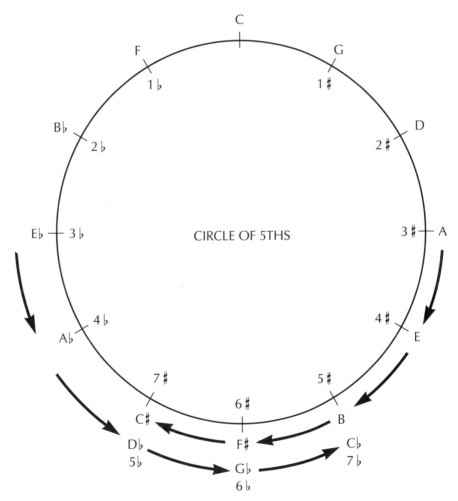

6 Write the required key signatures. Be careful to observe the exact left-to-right position of the sharps or flats. Before proceeding, review the correct way to notate a sharp and a flat by hand on p. 30.

G   D   A   E   B   F♯   C♯

F   B♭   E♭   A♭   D♭   G♭   C♭

7 Fill in the blank spaces, as in the completed example.

Ex. The key signature of D major uses _____**2 sharps**_____. In order, they are _____**F♯, C♯**_____.

a. The key signature of B♭ major uses _____. In order, they are _____.

b. C major uses _____. In order, they are _____.

c. A major uses _____. In order, they are _____.

d. E major uses _____. In order, they are _____.

e. The key signature of five sharps identifies the key of _____. In order, the sharps are

_____.

f. The key signature of four flats identifies the key of _____. In order, the flats are

_____.

g. The key signature of one flat identifies the key of _____. The flat is _____.

h. The key signature of one sharp identifies the key of _____. The sharp is _____.

i. The key signature of seven sharps identifies the key of _____. In order, they are

_____.

j. The key signature of seven flats identifies the key of _____. In order, they are

_____.

k. The key signature of six flats identifies the key of _____. In order, they are

_____.

l. The key signature of three flats identifies the key of _____. In order, they are

_____.

Transposition

In exercise #1 (p. 63), we shifted the beginning of a melody from one key to another in order to show the usefulness of key signatures. This process of shifting music from one key to another is called **transposition**, and it has many practical values in music. For instance, if you find that a certain song in the key of D major is too high for your voice, you can transpose it to a lower key in order to sing it. Transposing also helps to develop proficiency in understanding the use and interrelationships of different keys.

In musical terms, we say that the melody in exercise #1 was **transposed** from the key of C major to the keys of D major and A♭ major by using accidentals and not key signatures. Now we will begin transposing by using key signatures (as in exercise #3, pp. 64–65), which, to repeat, are *always* written at the beginning of every staff line. Once the key signature is written, it is no longer necessary to write sharps or flats before those notes that are represented in the key signature.

8 Observe the steps for transposing this melody from F major to A major, keeping intervals and scale degrees in mind.

Step 1: Write the new key signature. Write the first note, making sure it is the same scale degree as the original.

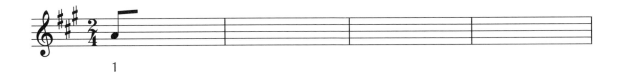

Step 2: Rewrite the music with exactly the same rhythm and the same order of intervals. Check to be sure that the scale degrees correspond.

9 a. Transpose the four measures of the melody in exercise #1a on p. 63 to the keys indicated below. Follow the steps for transposition shown above:

up to G

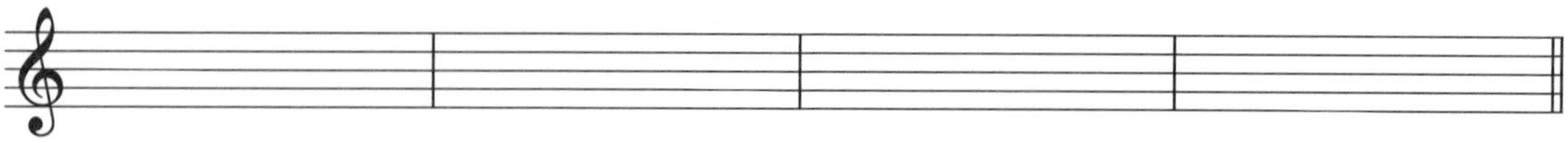

up to E♭

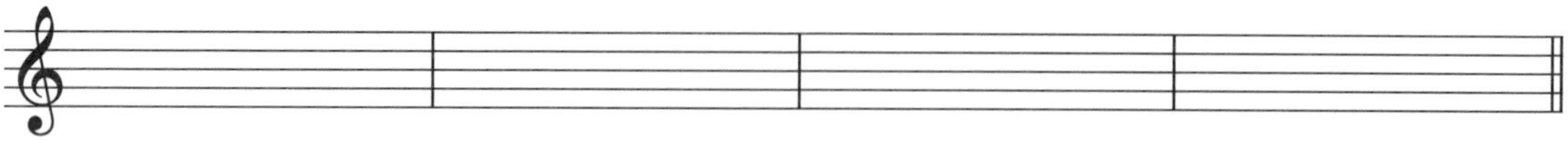

up to E

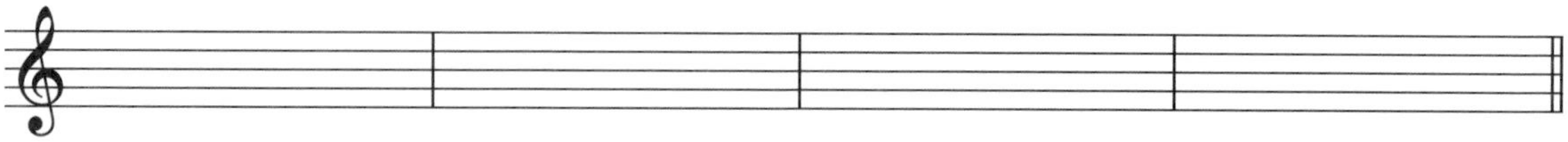

b. Transpose the first eight measures of Beethoven's *Ode to Joy* (*Scorebook* 59) to the indicated keys:

down to C

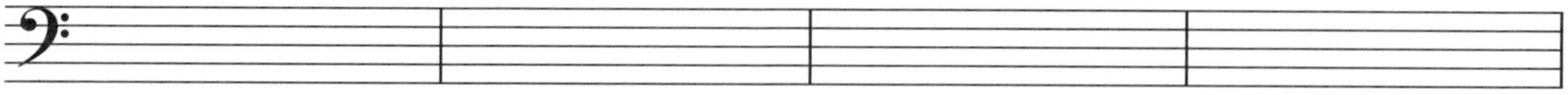

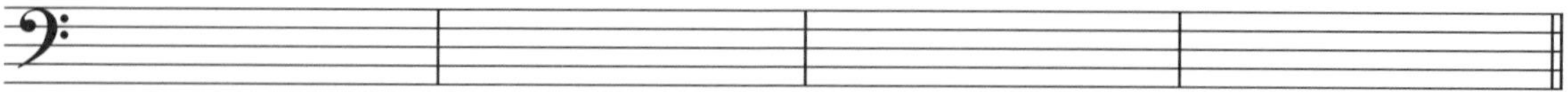

up to F

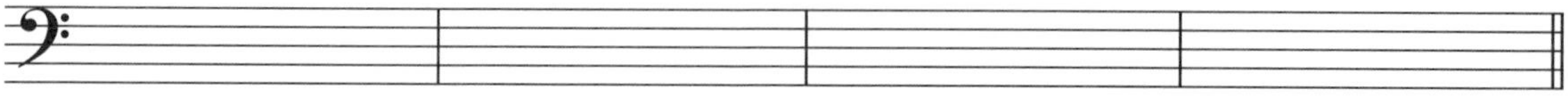

c. Transpose Brahms' *Lullaby* (*Scorebook* 55) through measure 8 to the indicated keys. Be sure to include the anacrusis* and then the next eight measures:

up to D

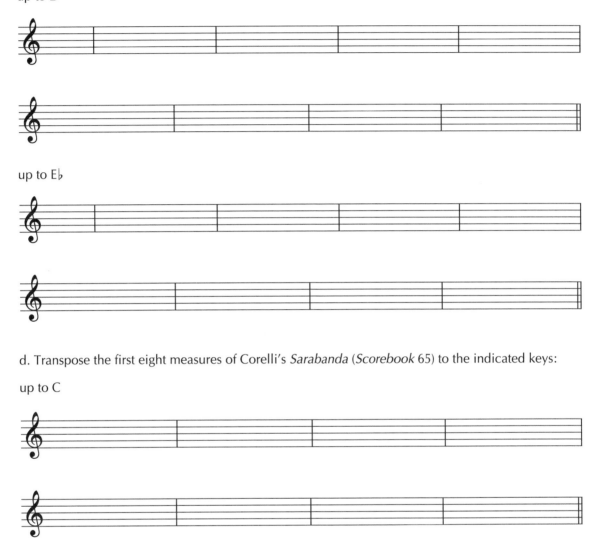

up to E♭

d. Transpose the first eight measures of Corelli's *Sarabanda* (*Scorebook* 65) to the indicated keys:

up to C

down to A♭

*The notes that occur at the beginning of a piece on the beat other than the first. (See *Rhythm Reader*, p. 27.)

Transposing Accidentals

If a melody contains a pitch that is not in the scale represented by the key signature, an accidental before that note is required. Observe in the example below, that the third note on the 4th scale degree has been raised one half step. When transposed, this note must also be raised one half step.

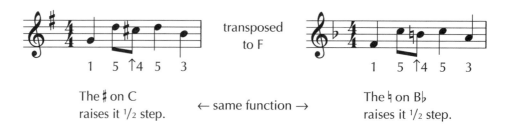

transposed to F

The ♯ on C raises it ½ step.

← same function →

The ♮ on B♭ raises it ½ step.

In this example, note that the accidental in the transposed melody is different from the accidental in the original melody. In the key of G, the accidental is a sharp. In the key of F, however, it is a natural. When transposing accidentals, *you cannot simply copy the original accidental.* Instead, you must consider the function of the original accidental.

> **TRANSPOSING ACCIDENTALS**
>
> When transposing an accidental, remember you are duplicating a function. Provide the corresponding accidental that functions in the same way as the original.

10 Transpose these examples. Indicate the function of the accidental (write "raise ½ step" or "lower ½ step"). Study the example carefully.

Example

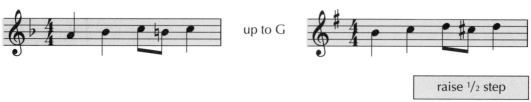

up to G

raise ½ step

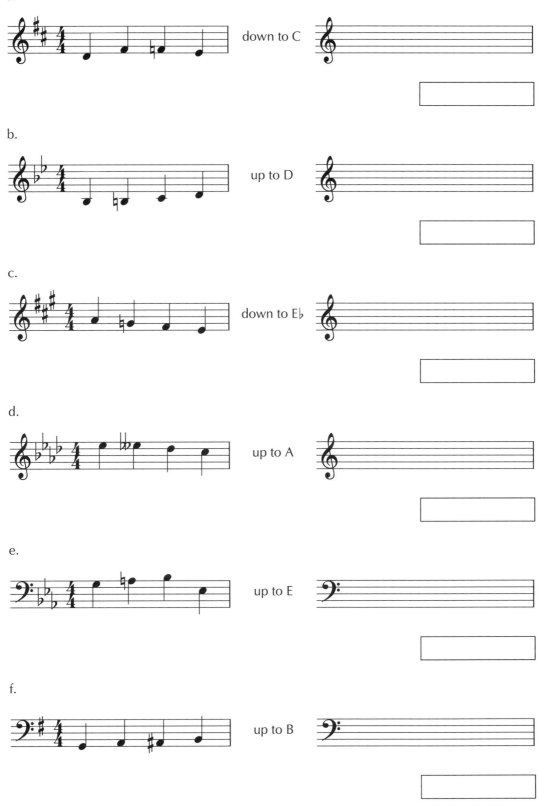

11   Transpose the following melody to the indicated keys. First write the correct key signature. Take care when transposing accidentals to remember the function that the original accidental performs. Notice the precautionary accidental.

down to B♭

up to D

up to E♭

down to F

Chromatic and Diatonic

Scales with major key signatures are diatonic. As we have discovered, transposing melodies with only diatonic pitches requires no accidentals. But what about melodies that do require accidentals on certain pitches? These notes lie outside of the diatonic scale and are called **chromatic notes**. Music that contains many chromatic notes is called chromatic music.

Melodic Organization

In Chapter Four, we learned a few of the basic components that make up melody: rhythm, intervals in succession, and steps, skips, and leaps in pitch. Let us now consider several other aspects of the way melody is organized: phrase and form, cadences, and melodic shape.

---

12 Listen to *The Water Is Wide* (Cassette). As you listen to the music, follow the text, given below, and notice how the various lines and verses of the song create a pattern.

> The water is wide, I cannot get o'er,
> And neither have I wings to fly.
> Give me a boat that can carry two,
> And both shall row, my love and I.
>
> I leaned my back against an oak,
> Thinking it was a trusty tree;
> But first it bended and then it broke,
> As thus did my true love to me.
>
> (Repeat first verse.)

Phrase and Form

Form describes the way music is organized, or put together. When listening to *The Water Is Wide*, we notice that the song is divided into *verses*, and that each verse displays a similar design, consisting of four lines of text and four **phrases** of music. A phrase is a musical statement leading to a pause or moment of rest, called a **cadence**. In this way, a musical phrase is very similar to a phrase of text. The form of one verse of *The Water Is Wide* can be diagrammed as follows:

phrase I
⌐────────────────────────────────────⌐ cadence

phrase II
⌐────────────────────────────────────⌐ cadence

phrase III
⌐────────────────────────────────────⌐ cadence

phrase IV
⌐────────────────────────────────────⌐ cadence

Words and Music

Another way to experience the form of a song is to speak the words without playing the music. Notice the rhyme scheme and flow of lines in each verse. Notice where the lines of poetry come to a point of rest. Now sing or listen to the song. Try to experience the interaction of words and music. We can describe a melody with words as sung poetry, where words and music form a unity.

13 Play (or have your instructor play) the following melodies. Consider the phrase-cadence design of each one.

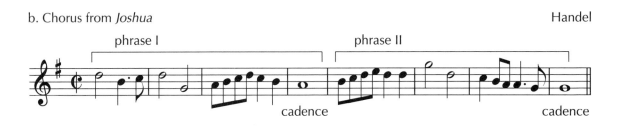

a.   German folk tune

b. Chorus from *Joshua*   Handel

The Cadence   When considering form, we are especially interested in **cadences**, the markers of phrase design. Identifying cadences, however, is not always easy. For example, you might think there is a cadence in exercise #13b at measure 2 because the second half note seems like a brief moment of rest. But this momentary pause is not a cadence, since it does not occur when the musical energy of the phrase is spent, or when the musical thought is completed. This happens in measures 4 and 8.

14 Examine the following melodies in the *Scorebook* for phrase and cadence. Mark cadences by lightly writing an apostrophe (') just after the note that ends each phrase.

> *Fray Diego*   (*Scorebook* 4)
> *Song of the Crow*   (*Scorebook* 10)

Melodic Shape   The characteristic way the intervals of a melody create a particular contour as the pitches move up and down can be described as **melodic shape**. The various patterns of melodic shape can be represented graphically by outlining the pitch direction of the melody.

15 Listen again to *The Water Is Wide* (Cassette), and follow the shape of each phrase shown in the pitch outline below.

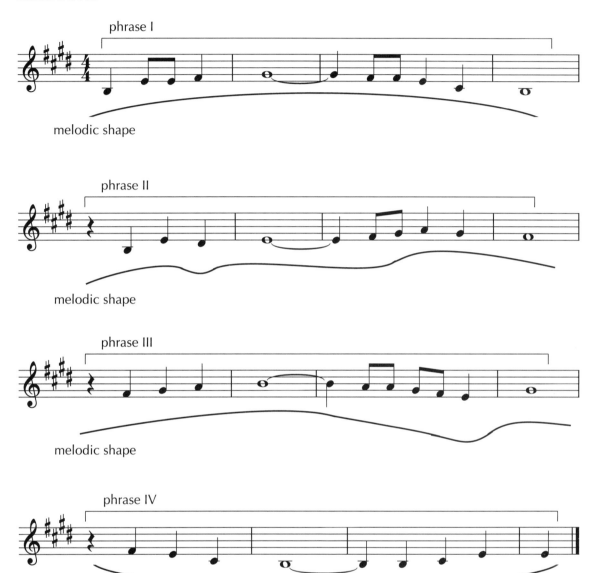

Phrase 1 of the melody follows a simple design, rising to a peak at the middle of the phrase and falling back at the end. Phrases II and III are more complex, with more curves toward the ends of the phrases. This relative complexity creates a feeling of ongoing activity, which pushes toward the last phrase. The concluding phrase outline is, once again, a simple design, a reflection of the first. Notice that the highest pitch of phrase II (A) is a step above the highest pitch of phrase I (G♯). Phrase III rises another step to B, the highest pitch in the song. In reaction to the rising shape of the first three phrases, the final phrase falls to B before rising to a cadence on the tonic, E.

16 Draw the melodic shape under the pitches of the following melodies.

a. *Wachet Auf*   J. S. Bach

b. Theme from *Symphony No. 103* (*Scorebook* 67)   Haydn

c. *Hunter's Theme* from *Der Freischütz* (*Scorebook* 70)   Weber

Composing a Melody

In Chapter Four, we considered tonality and various types of melodic movement (step, skip, and leap). In this chapter, we have learned about form, phrase, cadence, and melodic shape. When composing melodies, it is wise to consider how each of these musical elements can be combined in a musically pleasing way.

Following a particular melodic shape to determine the sequence of pitches is one way to start composing. You should, however, use this method in a flexible manner. While the shape of a melody is important, ultimately the ear guides the composer when choosing each note. Think of melodic shape as a guideline that can be altered where needed.

17 Using the indicated melodic shapes as a general plan, compose two two-phrase melodies, using notes from the C-major scale for one and notes from the F-major scale for the other. For each melody, end the *second* phrase on the tonic. Use *mostly* stepwise motion, limiting the number of skips and leaps.

a. C-major melody:

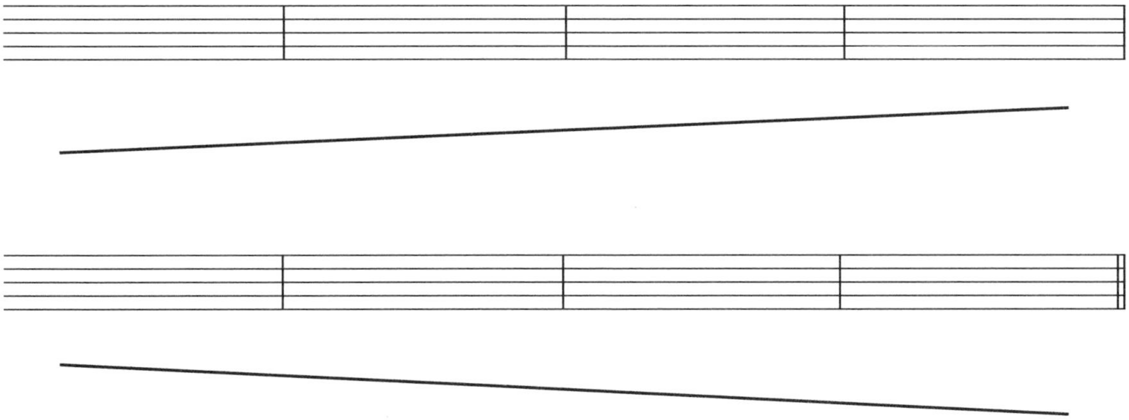

b. F-major melody:

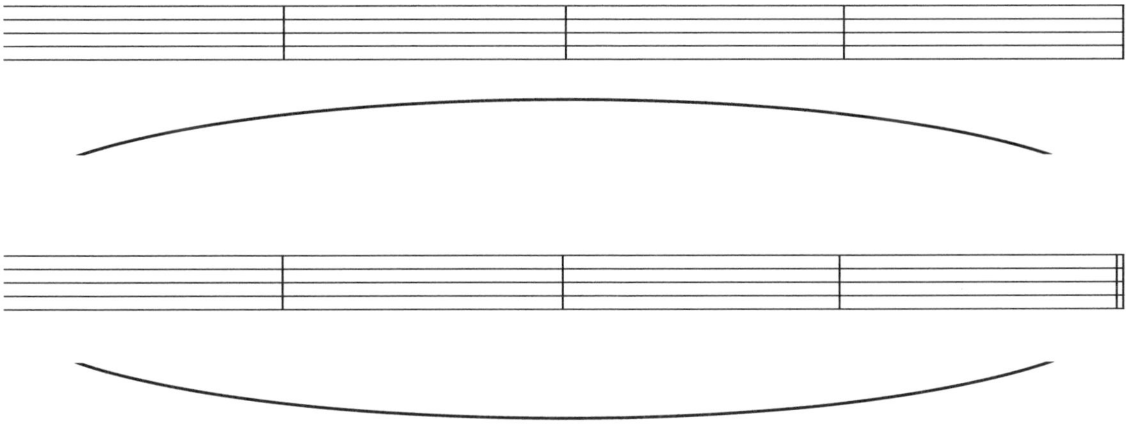

Singing Major-Scale Melodies

Various methods are used to sing major-scale melodies. Two of these are singing with numbers and singing with syllables. Both share a common purpose, to distinguish individual degrees of the major scale. To explore singing melodies in more detail, turn to Appendix III on page 240.

18 a. Sing the C-major scale up and down, first with numbers and then with syllables. Listen for the characteristic sound of each scale degree.

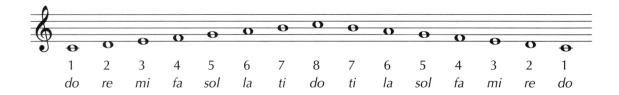

b. Sing the following melody, first with numbers and then with syllables.

TERMS, SYMBOLS, AND CONCEPTS

key signatures
circle of 5ths
transposition
transposing accidentals
chromatic
form

phrase
cadence
melodic shape
singing major scale melodies with
     numbers or syllables

SUGGESTED ACTIVITIES

1. Transpose the following melodies from the *Scorebook*.

   Game Song (*Scorebook* 3) to A major

   Die Gedanken sind frei (*Scorebook* 9) to C major

   Morley, *Nancie* (*Scorebook* 61) to E major

   Haydn, Theme from *Symphony No. 103* (*Scorebook* 67) to D major

   Mozart, Theme from *Symphony No. 29* (*Scorebook* 69) to B♭ major

2. Examine the following melodies in the *Scorebook* for phrases and cadences.

   Brahms, *Lullaby* (*Scorebook* 55)

   Hymn (Armenian) (*Scorebook* 22)

   O du schöner Rosengarten (*Scorebook* 5)

3. Draw the melodic shape of the following melodies from the *Scorebook*.

   O du schöner Rosengarten (*Scorebook* 5)

   Mozart, Theme from *Symphony No. 29* (*Scorebook* 69)

   Mozart, Theme from *Don Giovanni* (*Scorebook* 60)

4. Compose a four-phrase melody in the key of D major. First draw a melodic shape as a general design. Be sure to end the last phrase on the tonic.

CHAPTER SIX

Intervals

No topic is more important than intervals for understanding our musical system. If we compare music with language, we can see that intervals are like words: they are the basic building blocks of musical structure in the same way that words are the basic building blocks of grammatical structure. Intervals are one foundation on which melody and harmony rest.

There are various methods for understanding intervals. Each has merit, but no one method can explain all musical situations. Therefore, we will learn several approaches to the study of intervals, which together will promote a deeper understanding of intervals than a study limited to one method. Because intervals can be somewhat tricky, consider each section in this chapter carefully, not only seeking the right answers but also thinking about the *underlying principles* that guide you to those answers. The effort will be worthwhile.

Staff Steps and Half Steps

In Chapter Four, we measured intervals in terms of staff steps. But counting staff steps alone cannot identify intervals exactly. If we look closely at some intervals on the staff and keyboard, we will see why this is so.

---

1 Examine the following intervals. Notice both the number of staff steps *and* half steps in each interval.

a.

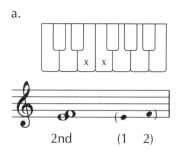

2nd   (1 2)

b.

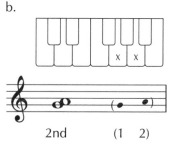

2nd   (1 2)

c.

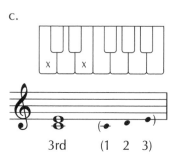

3rd   (1 2 3)

d.

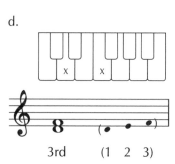

3rd   (1 2 3)

When we compare the 2nds above, we can see that interval a contains one half step and interval b contains two half steps. Both are 2nds, but interval b is *larger by one half step.* When we compare the 3rds, we note that interval c contains four half steps and interval d contains three. Both are 3rds, but interval d is *smaller by one half step.*

2 In each pair of intervals, count the number of half steps. Write the number in the blank provided below the staff. Circle the larger interval. Then name the interval by number of staff steps, and write it in the box above the diagram. Study the example carefully.

Example:

half steps **4**   half steps **3**

a.

half steps 5   half steps 6

b.

half steps 9   half steps _____

c.

half steps _____   half steps _____

d.

half steps _____   half steps _____

Interval Quality

The examples above illustrate that an interval may have the same number of staff steps as another but not be exactly the same size. These intervals can be distinguished one from the other in terms of interval **quality**. We use the following labels (and their abbreviations) to describe interval quality: **major** (M), **minor** (m), **perfect** (P), **augmented** (aug or A), **diminished** (dim or d).

In order to measure any interval with complete accuracy, you must use one of the designations of interval quality and the staff-step number. Now compare the following intervals with those in exercise #1 (p. 84):

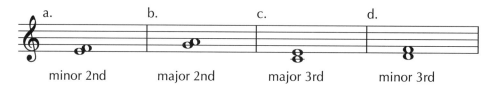

     minor 2nd   major 2nd   major 3rd   minor 3rd

WHICH QUALITY APPLIES?

1. **Major** and **minor** qualify 2nds, 3rds, 6ths, and 7ths.
2. **Perfect**, **augmented**, and **diminished** qualify 4ths and 5ths.
3. **Perfect** also qualifies unisons and octaves.

RELATIONSHIPS OF QUALITY DESIGNATIONS

1. A major interval is one half step *larger* than a minor interval.
2. An augmented interval is one half step *larger* than a perfect interval.
3. A diminished interval is one half step *smaller* than a perfect interval.

One way we can get to know the qualities of particular intervals is to memorize the number of half steps in each one. The following chart, which gives these numbers, can be used as a handy reference throughout this book.

Interval Half Steps

Interval	Abbreviation	Half steps	Interval	Abbreviation	Half steps
unison		0	perfect 5th	(P5)	7
minor 2nd	(m2)	1	augmented 5th	(aug5)	8
major 2nd	(M2)	2	minor 6th	(m6)	8
minor 3rd	(m3)	3	major 6th	(M6)	9
major 3rd	(M3)	4	minor 7th	(m7)	10
perfect 4th	(P4)	5	major 7th	(M7)	11
augmented 4th	(aug4)	6	octave	(P8)	12
diminished 5th	(dim5)	6			

The intervals given in the chart above are those most commonly found in tonal music. Later in this chapter, we will examine situations in which the qualifying terms "augmented" and "diminished" apply to other intervals besides the 4th and 5th. For the moment, let us learn these most common intervals.

3 Play and study each of the following intervals. Write the number of half steps in the box below the staff. Mark each note on the keyboard diagram.

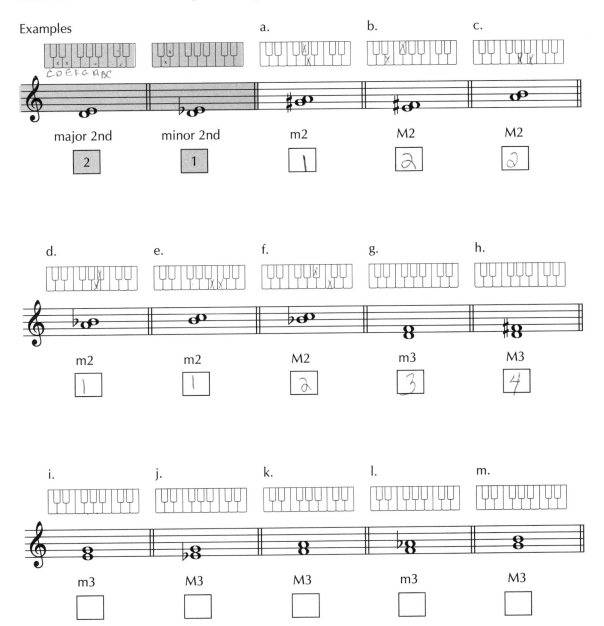

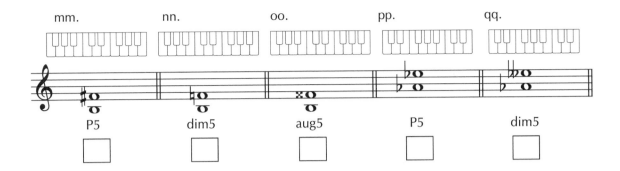

mm.   nn.   oo.   pp.   qq.

P5   dim5   aug5   P5   dim5

☐   ☐   ☐   ☐   ☐

4   Complete the following sentences.

a. Intervals containing the same number of staff steps but a different number of semitones are differentiated by _____.

b. 2nds, 3rds, 6ths, and 7ths are qualified by the terms _____.

c. 4ths and 5ths are qualified by the terms _____.

d. Major is one half step _____ than minor.

e. All major 3rds contain (the same, a different) _____ number of half steps.

f. All 3rds on the white keys contain (the same, a different _____ number of half steps.

g. All minor 2nds contain (the same, a different) _____ number of half steps.

h. All 2nds on the white keys contain (the same, a different) _____ number of half steps.

Intervals Within the Major Scale

Another way to recognize interval quality is through its association with the major scale. Play:

Key of C major

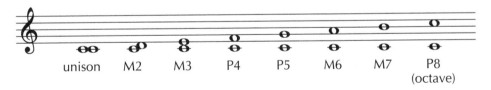

unison   M2   M3   P4   P5   M6   M7   P8 (octave)

Key of D major

(precautionary accidentals included)

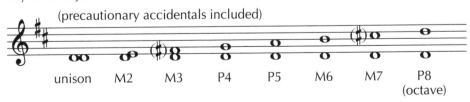

unison   M2   M3   P4   P5   M6   M7   P8 (octave)

Key of B♭ major

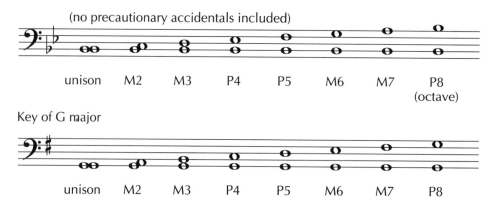

(no precautionary accidentals included)

unison　　M2　　M3　　P4　　P5　　M6　　M7　　P8
(octave)

Key of G major

unison　　M2　　M3　　P4　　P5　　M6　　M7　　P8
(octave)

MAJOR-SCALE INTERVAL RULES

The intervals of the major scale between the tonic and each of the other scale degrees are as follows:

1. 2nds, 3rds, 6ths, and 7ths are always major.
2. Unisons, 4ths, 5ths, and octaves are always perfect.
3. There are no minor intervals.

---

5 Complete the following sentences.

a. The interval from the tonic to the 3rd of a major scale is a _____.

b. The interval from the tonic to the 7th of a major scale is a _____.

c. The interval from the tonic to the 4th of a major scale is a _____.

d. The interval from the tonic to the 2nd of a major scale is a _____.

e. A major 7th above G is (name the exact note) _____.

f. A major 7th above B♭ is _____.

g. A major 2nd above G is _____.

h. A perfect 5th above B♭ is _____.

i. A major 3rd above D is _____.

j. A major 6th above C is _____.

k. A perfect 4th above G is _____.

l. A perfect 4th above D is _____.

m. In a major scale, the intervals from the tonic up to each scale degree can be major or perfect but never _____.

Altering Major-Scale Intervals

Major-scale intervals can be altered to form smaller or larger intervals by adding accidentals. Study the examples below:

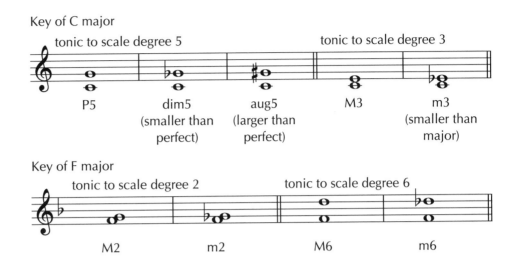

Key of C major

tonic to scale degree 5   tonic to scale degree 3

P5   dim5   aug5   M3   m3
      (smaller than   (larger than   (smaller than
      perfect)   perfect)   major)

Key of F major

tonic to scale degree 2   tonic to scale degree 6

M2   m2   M6   m6

---

6 Name the major key for each staff in the box provided. Then name the 2nds, 3rds, 6ths, and 7ths. The intervals within the major scale of the indicated key are all major and have no accidentals other than the sharps or flats found in the key signature. An interval that is a half step smaller than major is minor and requires an accidental. Play each interval.

Remember that the key signature at the beginning of each staff applies to the entire staff; the double bar does not change the key signature. Remember also that an accidental applies only to notes in the measure in which it first appears.

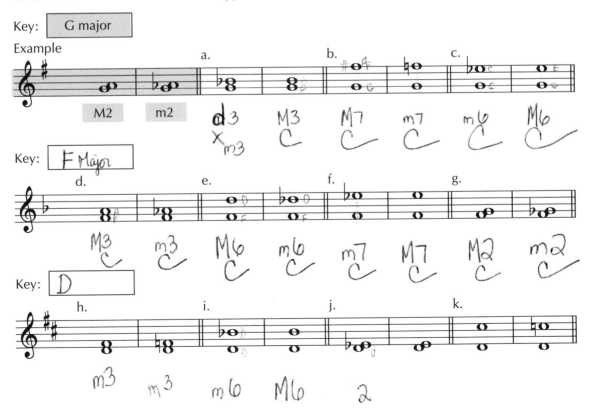

Key: [G major]

Example   a.   b.   c.

M2   m2   d3   M3   M7   m7   m6   M6
          ×m3

Key: [F Major]

d.   e.   f.   g.

M3   m3   M6   m6   m7   M7   M2   m2

Key: [D]

h.   i.   j.   k.

m3   m3   m6   M6   2

Key: Bb Major

Key: A

Key:

Key:

Key:

7 Name these 4ths and 5ths. Intervals within the major scale will be perfect. Intervals a half step larger than perfect will be augmented. Intervals a half step smaller than perfect will be diminished. Play each interval. Study the example carefully.

Example

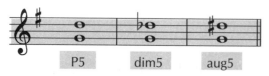

8 Complete the following statements. Include the interval quality in your answers.

Ex. In the key of G major, the tonic is ___G___ and the 3rd scale degree is ___B___. The resulting

interval is a ___M3___.

a. In the key of B♭ major, the tonic is _____ and the 2nd scale degree is _____. The resulting

   interval is a _____.

b. In the key of A♭ major, the 5th scale degree is _____. The interval from tonic to 5 is a _____.

c. In the key of D major, the 7th scale degree is _____. The interval from tonic to 7 is a _____.

d. In the key of B major, the 3rd scale degree is _____. The interval from 1 to 3 is a _____.

e. In the key of E♭ major, the 7th degree is _____. The interval from 1 to 7 is a _____.

f. In the key of E major, the 6th degree is _____. The interval from 1 to 6 is a _____.

g. In the key of D♭ major, the 3rd degree is _____. The interval from 1 to 3 is a _____.

h. In the key of F major, the 4th degree is _____. The interval from 1 to 4 is a _____.

i. In the key of C♯ major, the 7th degree is _____. The interval from 1 to 7 is a _____.

Limitations of the Major-Scale Method

Many musicians have learned intervals by associating them with the major scale. But this method has one important limitation. Suppose you are playing a piece in Ab major and want to identify an interval whose lower note is F. Do you start thinking in the key of F? The answer is no; but this situation demonstrates the need for a variety of approaches to the study of intervals. We will now consider a method for determining intervallic distances when the lower note of a major-scale interval is not the tonic.

The Natural Semitones

A common pitfall in the study of intervals is that *many intervals look alike but are not always the same size.* In Chapter Two, we learned that knowledge of the keyboard is essential to understanding our musical system. In the following discussion of intervals, we will see how the construction of the keyboard and the position of the two semitones on the white keys affect interval quality.

9   Play each interval. Identify it as a half step (m2) or whole step (M2). Use the keyboard as a reference.

M2

Notice that the only half steps (minor 2nds) on the white keys occur between E and F and between B and C. We will refer to these as half steps the **natural semitones**, since they are the only semitones that do not use a black key.

NATURAL SEMITONES

E–F and B–C are the only two natural semitones. On the keyboard, they are the only white keys that have no black key between them.

The Natural Intervals

Natural intervals are those in which both notes have no accidentals and fall on white keys of the piano. We can determine the size of a natural interval by identifying the number and type of natural whole and half steps it contains.

10 Compare the following pairs of intervals. Using small-sized quarter noteheads, write in and identify the natural seconds contained within each interval, as shown in the example. Use "1" for whole step and "¹/₂" for half step.

Example:

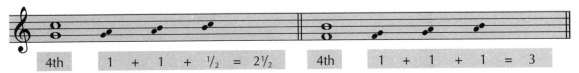

a.

b.

c.

d.

In exercise #10a, both intervals are 3rds; but the first (G–B) contains two whole steps, while the second (A–C) contains one whole step and one half step. Therefore, the second interval is smaller *although both intervals look the same on the staff.*

11   Play and study the following natural intervals.

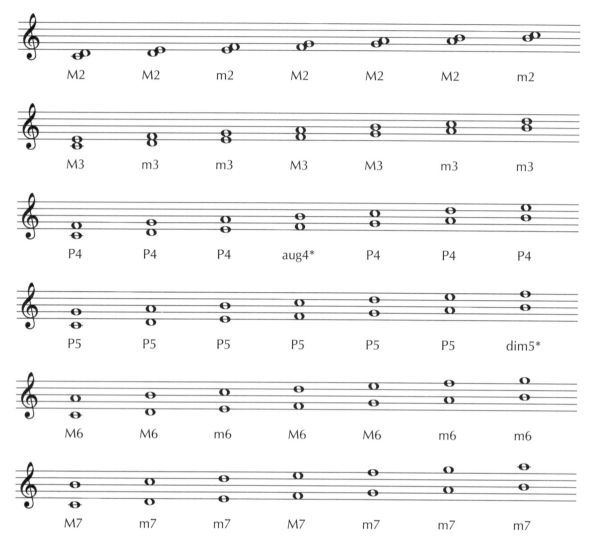

M2	M2	m2	M2	M2	M2	m2
M3	m3	m3	M3	M3	m3	m3
P4	P4	P4	aug4*	P4	P4	P4
P5	P5	P5	P5	P5	P5	dim5*
M6	M6	m6	M6	M6	m6	m6
M7	m7	m7	M7	m7	m7	m7

*Notice that F–B (aug4) and B–F (dim5) are inversions of each other.

RULES FOR NATURAL INTERVALS

2nds: Natural 2nds are *major* except for E–F and B–C, which are the natural semitones and therefore *minor*.

3rds: Natural 3rds containing one of the natural semitones are *minor*; the other 3rds, which contain neither of the natural semitones, are *major*.

4ths: All natural 4ths *except* F–B contain one of the natural semitones and are *perfect*. Since F-B contains neither of the natural semitones, it is *augmented*.

5ths: All natural 5ths *except* B–F contain one of the natural semitones and are *perfect*. Since B–F contains two natural semitones, it is *diminished*.

Remember that F–B (aug4) and B–F (dim5) are inversions of each other.

6ths and 7ths: If a 6th or 7th contains one of the natural semitones, it is *major*; if it contains the two natural semitones, it is *minor*.

Adding Accidentals

You can use what you know about natural intervals when identifying intervals that use accidentals. Simply relate the given interval back to its natural spelling. Study the following examples carefully.

1. If you *raise* or lower *both* notes of an interval the same distance, the quality of the interval remains the same.

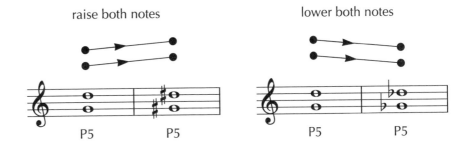

2. If you *raise* only the *higher* note of the interval, the interval *increases* in size.

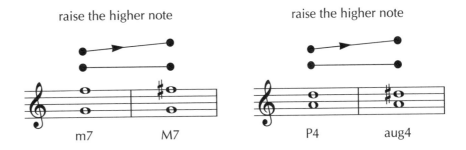

3. If you *raise* only the *lower* note of an interval, the interval *decreases* in size.

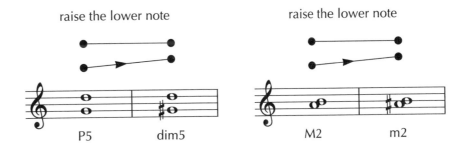

4. If you *lower* only the *higher* note of an interval, the interval *decreases* in size.

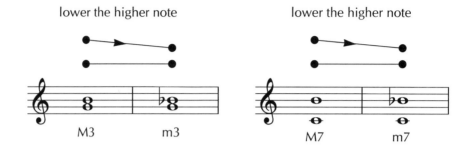

5. If you *lower* only the *lower* note of an interval, the interval *increases* in size.

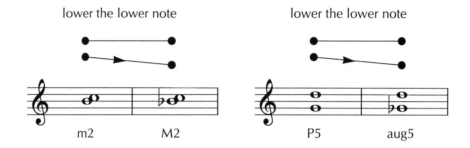

12 Complete the following statements. Refer to the examples above.

a. If you lower the higher note of an interval, it _____ in size.

b. If you lower the lower note of an interval, it _____ in size.

c. If you raise both notes of an interval the same distance, the quality of the interval

_____.

d. If you lower both notes of an interval the same distance, the quality of the interval

_____.

e. If you raise the lower note of an interval, it _____ in size.

f. If you raise the higher note of an interval, it _____ in size.

g. A minor 3rd is one half step _____ than a major 3rd.

h. A major 6th is one half step _____ than a minor 6th.

i. A diminished 5th is one half step _____ than a perfect 5th.

j. An augmented 4th is one step _____ than a perfect 4th.

13 Cover the accidentals in the following intervals with your finger. First consider each interval with no accidentals, and think of the interval's name. Then lift your finger and name the interval by determining whether it has increased or decreased in size or remained the same. Write the correct name under each interval.

ss.   tt.   uu.   vv.   ww.   xx.   yy.   zz.

Quality of Inverted Intervals

In Chapter Four you learned how to identify and construct inverted intervals by noting that the number of the original interval and its inversion always add up to the number 9. The quality of intervals is also affected when they are inverted, and can be summed up by the following rules: a perfect interval will always remain perfect. For example, the inversion of a perfect fifth is a perfect fourth. Major and minor intervals reverse their quality. For instance, the inversion of a minor 2nd is a major 7th, and the inversion of a major 3rd is a minor 6th. Diminished and augmented intervals also reverse their quality. For example, the inversion of a diminished 5th is an augmented 4th.

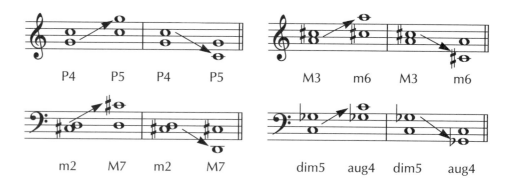

P4   P5   P4   P5   M3   m6   M3   m6

m2   M7   m2   M7   dim5   aug4   dim5   aug4

INVERTED INTERVAL QUALITY

1. Inversions of perfect intervals remain perfect.
2. Inversions of major intervals become minor, and minor intervals become major.
3. Inversions of diminished intervals become augmented, and augmented intervals become diminished.

Other Applications of Diminished and Augmented

The terms "diminished" and "augmented" can also apply to 2nds, 3rds, 6ths, and 7ths, although these usages are encountered less frequently. (Augmented and diminished octaves and unisons are rarer still.) In the diagram below, note how augmented intervals are one half step larger than major intervals, and diminished intervals are one half step smaller than minor intervals:

M2   aug2   m3   dim3   M6   aug6   m7   dim7

We will encounter important uses of the augmented 2nd and the diminished 7th in later chapters. Therefore, it is important to understand now how they are constructed.

A SUMMARY OF ALL INTERVAL FUNCTIONS

1. Most 2nds, 3rds, 6ths, and 7ths are either **major** or **minor**. However, **diminished** and **augmented** versions of these intervals occur occasionally.
2. **Perfect, augmented,** and **diminished** identify unisons, 4ths, 5ths, and 8ves (octaves). **Major** and **minor** *never* describe 4ths, 5ths, unisons, or 8ves.
3. **Major** is one half step *larger* than **minor**.
4. **Augmented** is one half step *larger* than **perfect**.
5. **Diminished** is one half step *smaller* than **perfect**.
6. When applied to 2nds, 3rds, 6ths, and 7ths, **diminished** is one half step *smaller* than **minor**, and **augmented** is one half step *larger* than **major**.

Consonance and Dissonance

When does music sound pleasing to our ear? When does it sound jarring? We use the terms **consonance** and **dissonance** to describe our perception of these properties of musical sound. Note the following descriptions:

Dissonant	**Consonant**
"active"	"at rest"
"unstable"	"stable"
"tense"	"relaxed"

When dissonant sounds move toward consonant sounds in a piece of music, they are said to *resolve*. Stated another way, when a dissonant sound is followed by a consonant sound the consonance is a *resolution* of the dissonance. The terms "consonant" and "dissonant" can also be applied to specific intervals. For example:

The perception of consonance and dissonance depends upon the musical context. In music of different historical periods or of different areas of the world, these perceptions are sometimes at odds with each other. It is important to think of these designations, therefore, as relative and flexible. In traditional Western music, 3rds, 5ths, 6ths, and octaves are considered consonant, and 2nds and 7ths, dissonant. Depending on the context, perfect 4ths seem either consonant or dissonant. The augmented 4th is usually considered one of the most dissonant intervals.

14   Play the following intervals. If an interval seems dissonant to you, mark it with a D. If an interval seems consonant, mark it with a C. If your are not sure, leave it alone. When a dissonance is followed by a consonance, write the word "resolves" between the two intervals. Name all the intervals. Note changes in clefs and key signatures.

Example:

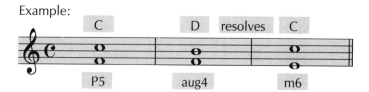

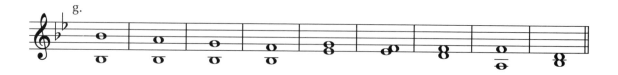

15 In the following example, play each interval. Be sure to hold the whole notes for an entire measure so that the interval is sounded. Name each interval. Circle only those intervals that sound dissonant. If in doubt, refer to the traditional classifications given above.

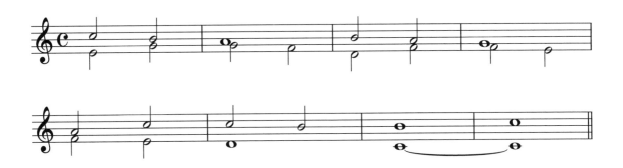

TERMS, SYMBOLS, AND CONCEPTS

interval quality
major-scale intervals
natural semitones
effect of the natural semitones on
    intervals

quality of inverted intervals
consonant
dissonant

SUGGESTED ACTIVITIES

1. Using the manuscript paper, copy the first four measures of the theme from Mozart's *Symphony No. 29* (*Scorebook* 69). Transpose it to G major. Name all intervals.
2. Examine *Christmas Has Come* (*Scorebook* 51). Look for any dissonances and their resolutions.

CHAPTER SEVEN

The Minor Scale

In the preceding chapters, we examined elements of music that are based on the major scale. Another scale that is widely used in Western music is the **minor scale**. Unlike the major scale, the minor scale takes three forms, each with a different pattern of whole and half steps. The most basic form is the **natural minor scale**. We will concentrate most of our discussion of minor scales on the natural minor (and take up the other two forms, harmonic minor and melodic minor, later in this chapter). Listen to *Dear Willie* (Cassette, *Scorebook* 30) to hear the natural minor scale's characteristic sound. We can see the natural minor scale's organization of half steps and whole steps by playing the white keys on the keyboard from A to A.

1 Play the A–natural minor scale.

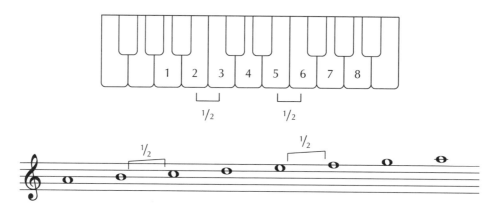

Natural Minor Scale Construction

In the natural minor scale, the half steps fall between scale degrees 2 and 3 and between 5 and 6; all other steps are whole steps. Compare this half-step/whole-step pattern with that of the major scale:

major scale: 1   2   3   4   5   6   7   8
                             └─┘   └─┘
                             ½   ½

natural minor scale: 1   2   3   4   5   6   7   8
                             └─┘   └─┘
                             ½   ½

Both the major scale and the natural minor scale are made up of two half steps and five whole steps. It is the placement of the two half steps that identifies the scale.

2 Write these natural minor scales on both the keyboard and staff, being careful to maintain the correct half-step/whole-step relationships. Draw the appropriate clef on each staff first. Bracket the half steps. For this exercise, use accidentals rather than key signatures.

Example: G natural minor

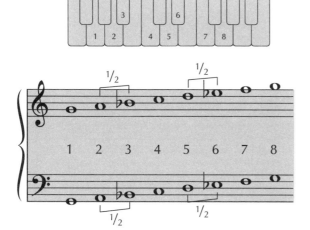

a. D natural minor

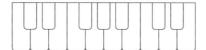

b. C natural minor

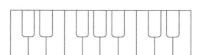

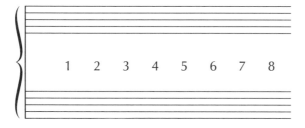

c. F natural minor

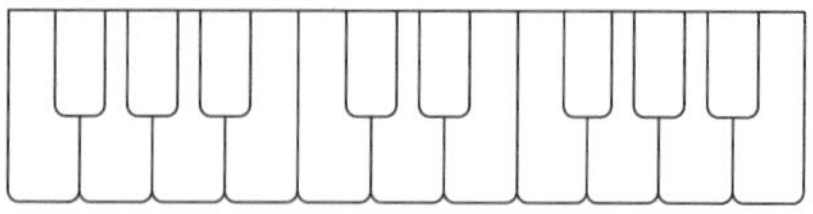

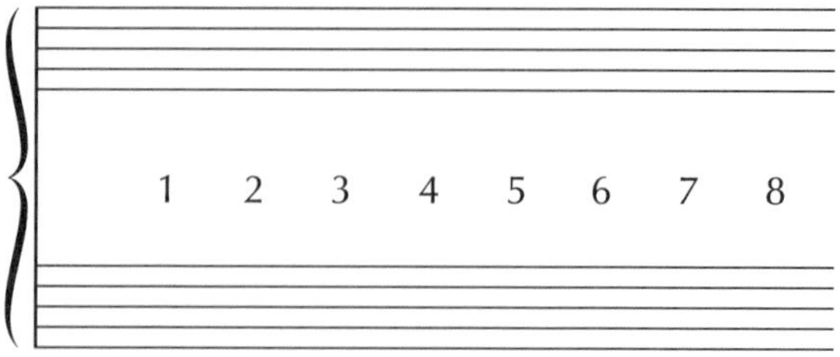

d. E natural minor

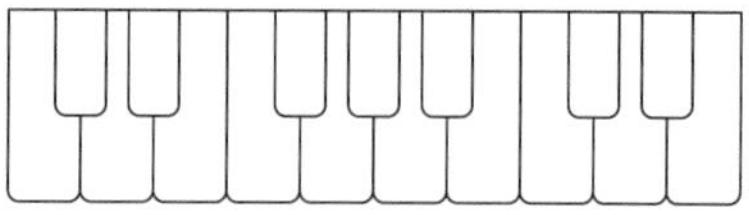

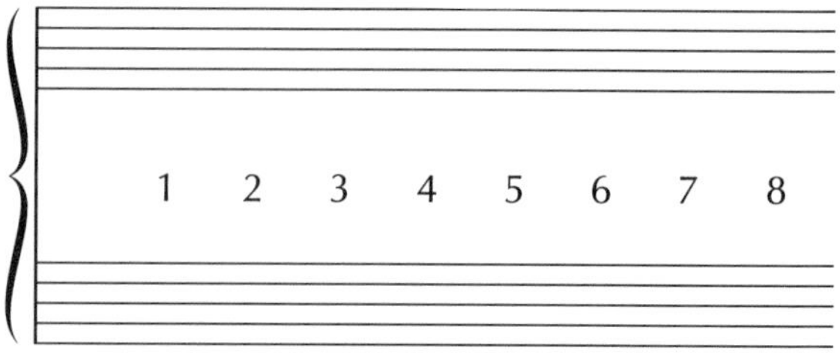

1 2 3 4 5 6 7 8

1 2 3 4 5 6 7 8

e. B natural minor

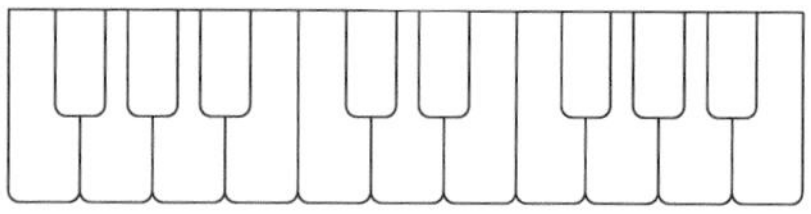

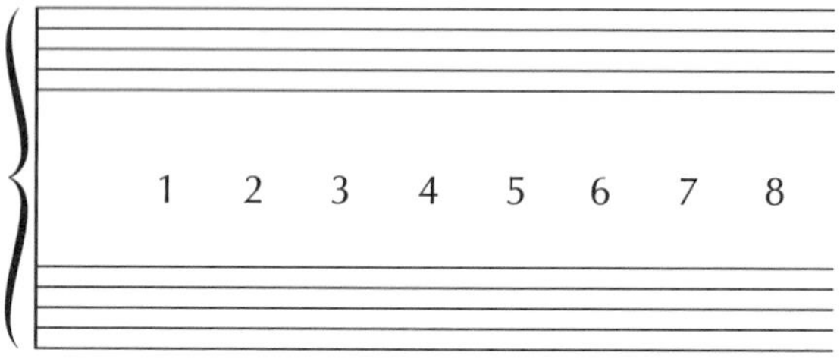

f. F♯ natural minor

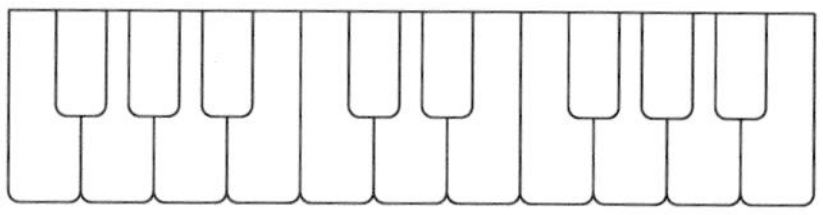

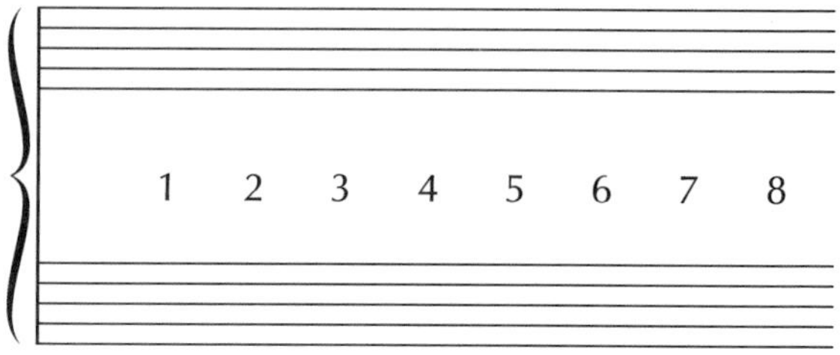

1 2 3 4 5 6 7 8

1 2 3 4 5 6 7 8

g. C♯ natural minor

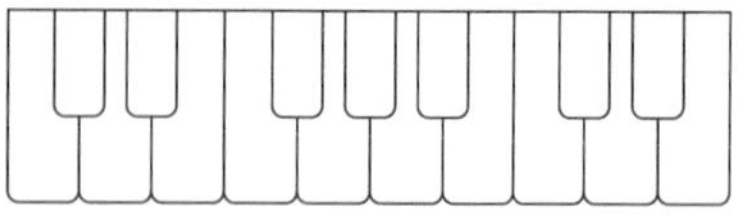

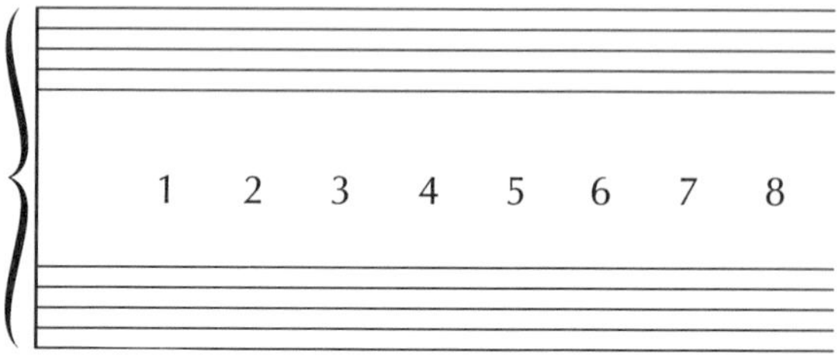

h. B♭ natural minor

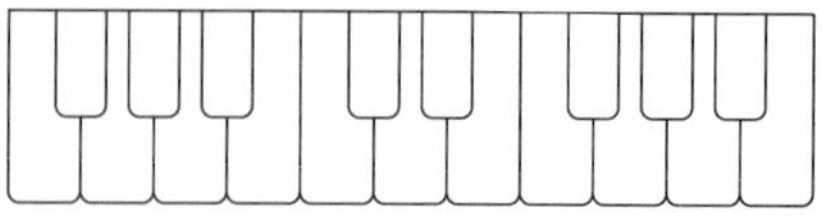

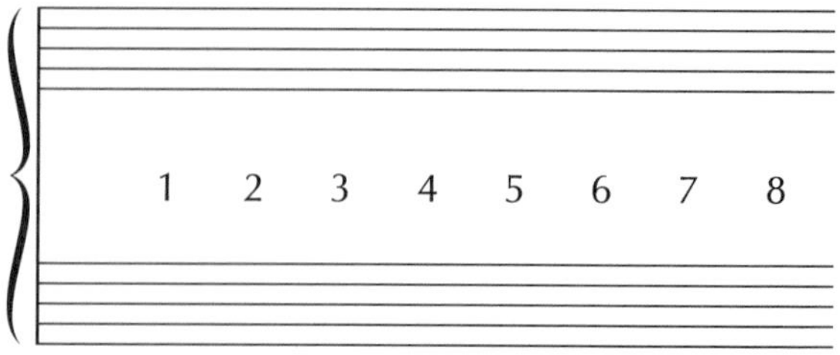

1 2 3 4 5 6 7 8

1 2 3 4 5 6 7 8

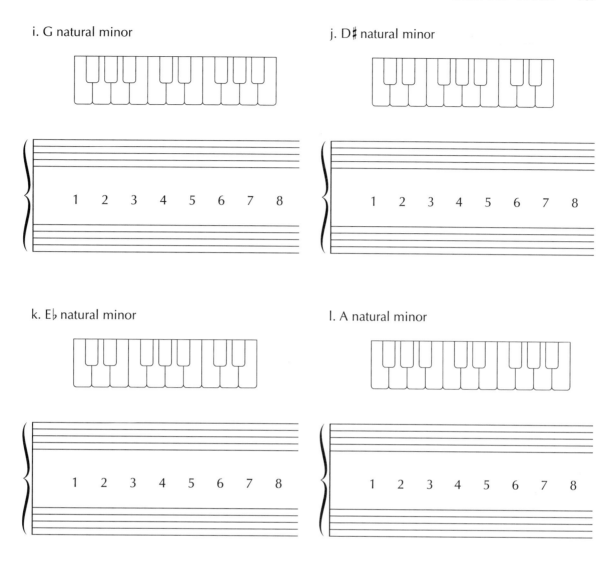

i. G natural minor

j. D♯ natural minor

1 2 3 4 5 6 7 8

1 2 3 4 5 6 7 8

k. E♭ natural minor

l. A natural minor

1 2 3 4 5 6 7 8

1 2 3 4 5 6 7 8

Other minor scales appear in Appendix II.

Minor-Scale Key Signatures

The key signatures for minor scales are related to those for the major scales. If we begin a major scale on its 6th scale degree instead of on the tonic, and then play the notes of the major scale upward until we reach the 6th scale degree an octave higher, we will have played a natural minor scale. Thus, a natural minor scale uses as its tonic pitch the major scale's 6th scale degree. Study this relationship in the following scales:

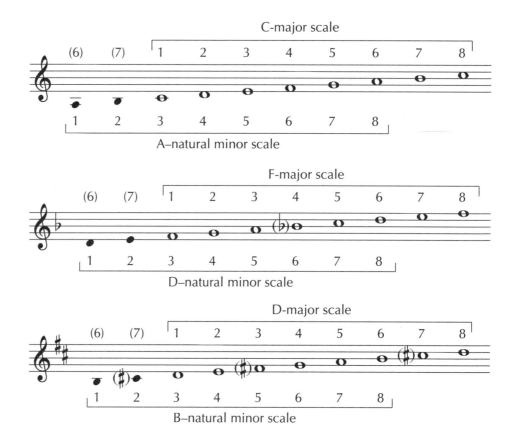

Relative Minor/ Relative Major

We can see that major and natural minor scales containing the same pitches but starting on different notes *have the same key signatures*. For instance, both the C-major and A-minor scales contain no flats or sharps, F major and D minor have one flat, and D major and B minor have two sharps. Because of the close relationship between A minor and C major, we say that A minor is the **relative minor** of C major, and conversely, that C major is the **relative major** of A minor. Similarly, the relative minor of F major is D minor, and the relative major of B minor is D major. (Notice that you can describe this relationship by starting with either the major or minor key.)

3 Complete the following sentences. Refer to the scales above, if necessary.

a. The natural minor scale contains the pitches of a major scale, but starts on the major scale's _____ degree.

b. Because the two scales are made up of the same pitches, they have the same _____.

c. A minor is called the _____ of C major.

d. C major is called the _____ of A minor.

e. The relative major scale of D minor is _____.

f. The relative minor key signature of B minor is the same as the major key signature of _____.

**Finding
the Relative
Minor Scale**

To find the relative minor scale of a specific major scale, start on the tonic of the major scale and go down an interval of a third within the scale. Notice that the 3rd is a minor 3rd (m3). This note is the *tonic* of the relative minor scale. Observe this process in the following example:

G-major scale

scale degree: 1   2   3   4   5   6   7   8

Go down a minor 3rd from G (three scale steps).

scale degree: 6   7   1   2   3   4   5   6   7   8

The relative minor is E minor.

scale degree: 1   2   3   4   5   6   7   8

**Finding
the Relative
Major Scale**

To find the relative major scale or key, simply reverse the process shown above: go up a minor 3rd (three scale steps) from the tonic of the natural minor scale to find the tonic of the relative major.

C-minor scale

1   2   3   4   5   6   7   8

Go up a minor 3rd (three scale steps).

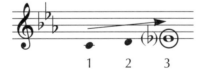

1   2   3

The relative major is E♭ major.

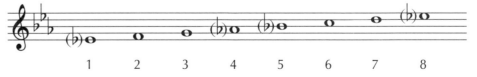

1   2   3   4   5   6   7   8

Minor-Scale Key Signatures / Circle of 5ths

We can now study all the minor key signatures first on the staff and then within the organization of the circle of 5ths (compare with pp. 68–69). This is a good opportunity to review all the major key signatures in addition to learning each relative minor.

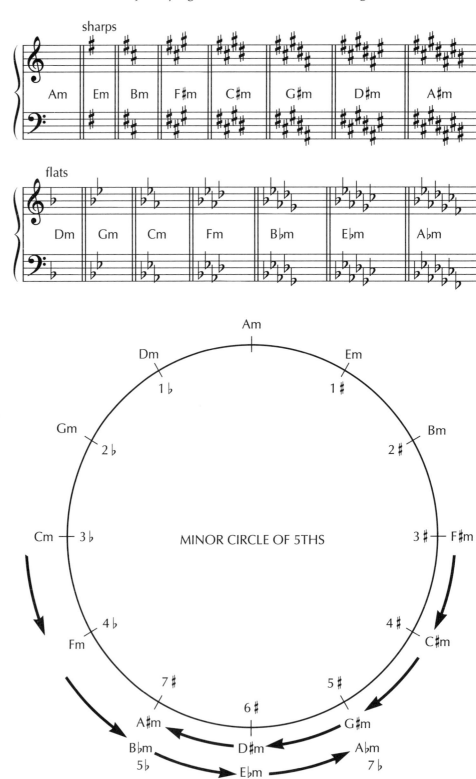

4 In the box provided, name the relative minor of the major keys given above the staff. Write out those relative minor scales in both clefs, complete with key signatures.

Example: F

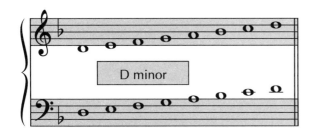

D minor

a. D   b. B♭

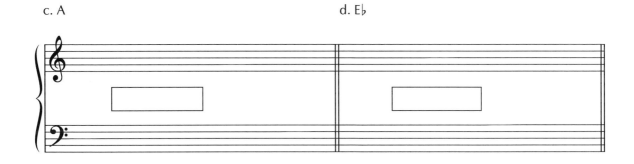

c. A   d. E♭

c. A   d. E♭

e. E   f. A♭

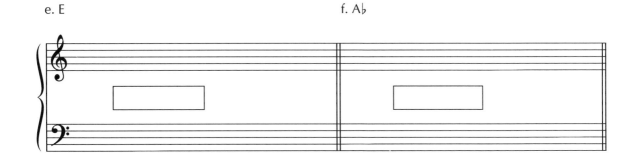

g. B   h. D♭

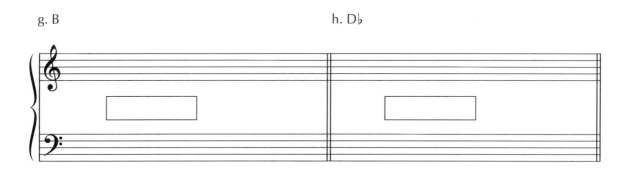

i. G   j. F♯

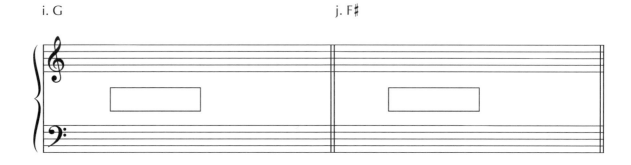

k. G♭   l. C♯

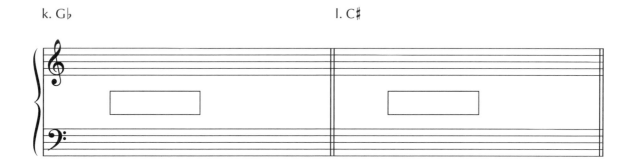

5   Name each of the following key signatures, first as a major key, then as a minor key.

Example   a.   b.   c.

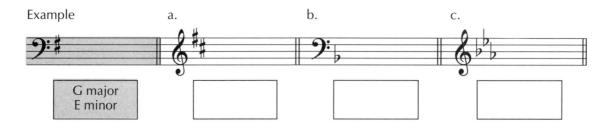

G major
E minor

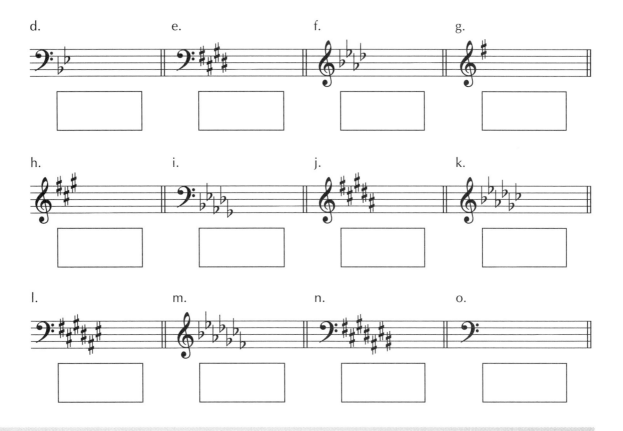

Parallel Minor/ Parallel Major

We have seen that relative major and minor scales share the same pitches and key signatures but begin on *different* notes. When major and minor scales begin on the *same* note, they are called **parallel**. For instance, the parallel minor key of C major is C minor, and the parallel major key of B minor is B major. Parallel major and minor scales differ from relative major and minor scales in two important ways: they do not share all the same notes, and they do not have the same key signatures.

6 Play and study each of these parallel major and minor scales. Notice the key signatures and the position of the half steps and whole steps.

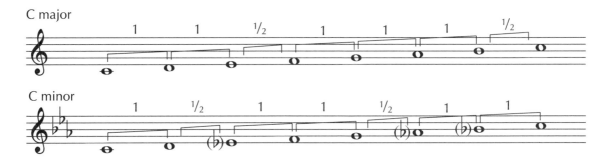

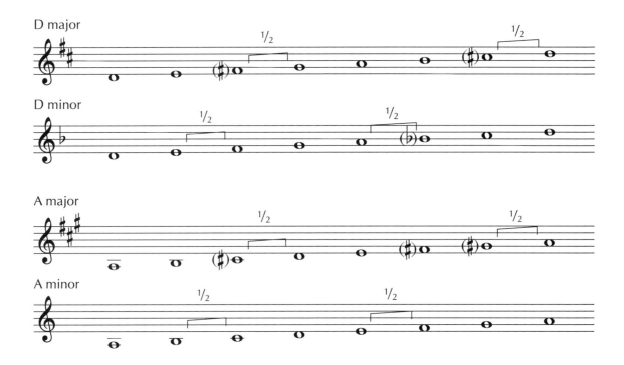

D major

D minor

A major

A minor

7 Construct the following parallel major/minor scales in the bass clef. Make sure you include key signatures. Label the half steps, and write the precautionary sharps or flats from the key signature in the scale, as in the examples above.

F major

F minor

The Relationship of Parallel Major to Minor

Because parallel keys share the same tonic and other important scale degrees, they are closely related in a tonal sense. A piece may shift to its parallel major or minor key with ease, since the basic tonality (key of the tonic) remains the same. Observe the change from G minor to G major in this excerpt:

Slavonic Dance, Op. 46, No. 8   Dvořák

Singing the Natural Minor Scale   The natural minor scale can be sung in several ways. Here we will learn the most convenient way: with numbers. You may refer to Appendix III, p. 240, for a discussion of how to sing the natural minor scale with syllables.

8   Sing the following natural minor scale with numbers.

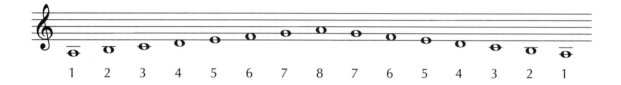

1   2   3   4   5   6   7   8   7   6   5   4   3   2   1

Other Forms of the Minor Scale   Two other forms of minor scales have evolved in our Western system, through the practice of altering certain pitches within the natural minor scale. One such alteration common to both of these minor scales involves raising the natural minor scale's 7th degree one half step. This raised 7th degree, called a **leading tone** because of its tendency to *lead into* the tonic, lies just one half step below the tonic. We will see in our study of harmony that the inclination of the leading tone to move toward the tonic is much greater than that of the natural minor scale's 7th scale degree, which lies farther away—one whole step below the tonic. The following examples demonstrate raised 7th degrees in minor scales (notice the use of an accidental to raise this scale step):

1.   *American folk tune*

Key: A minor   leading   leading
                        tone   tone

2. *Minuet* (*Scorebook* 64)   Visée

Key: D minor

3. *Fugue in C Minor*   J. S. Bach

Key: C minor

The Harmonic Minor Scale

The **harmonic minor scale** can be created from the natural minor scale simply by raising its 7th scale degree. All the other notes remain the same.

E natural minor   E harmonic minor

9   Play the following scales. Notice that one scale requires the addition of a sharp to create the leading tone, while the other requires a natural. Both accidentals perform *the same function*: that of raising the 7th degree one half step.

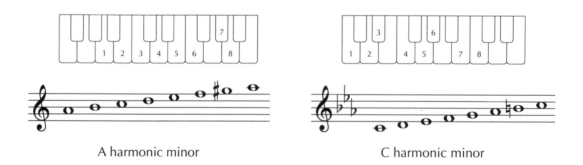

A harmonic minor   C harmonic minor

The Augmented 2nd

In each of the harmonic minor scales given above, there is a 2nd containing three semitones. We saw in Chapter Six that this interval is called an **augmented 2nd**, that is, a 2nd that is *one half step larger* than a major 2nd. The augmented 2nd is a feature of all harmonic minor scales, since by raising the 7th scale degree one half step to create the leading tone, the interval between scale degrees 6 and 7 become one half step larger. Observe the augmented 2nd in the following harmonic minor scale:

10   Bracket the augmented 2nds in the following harmonic scales. Then write the interval as a *harmonic* augmented 2nd (refer to harmonic intervals in Chapter Four, p. 57). Indicate all accidentals of the interval, even if they appear in the key signature. Study the example carefully.

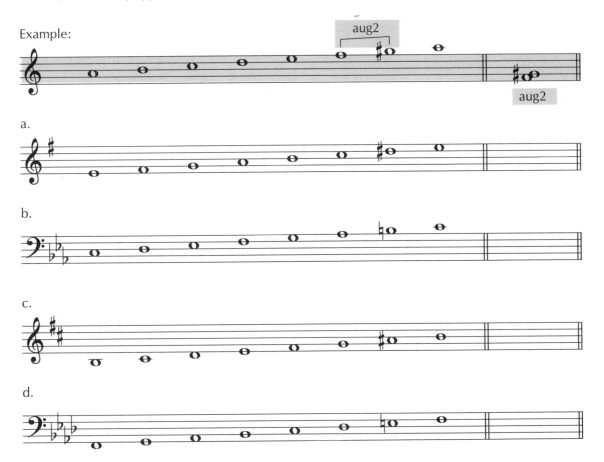

11 Write these harmonic minor scales on the keyboard and on the staff. Use both clefs of the grand staff. Include key signatures.

Example: A harmonic minor

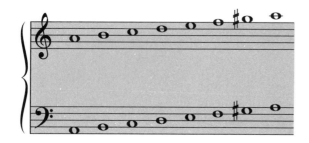

a. E harmonic minor

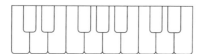

b. G harmonic minor

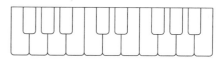

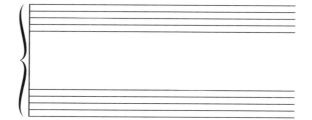

c. D harmonic minor

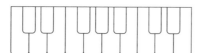

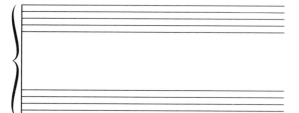

d. F harmonic minor

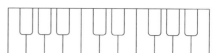

e. B harmonic minor

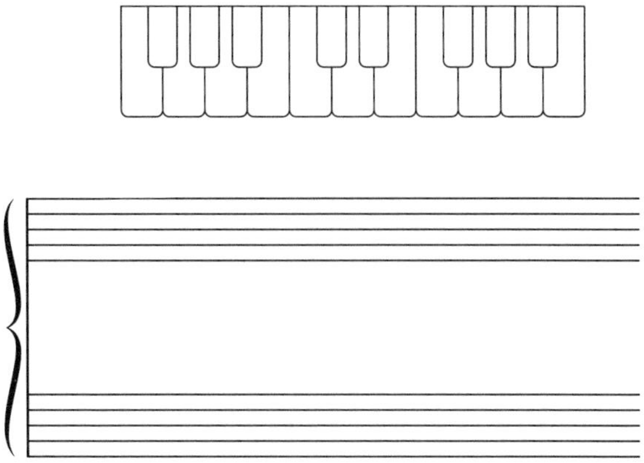

f. C harmonic minor

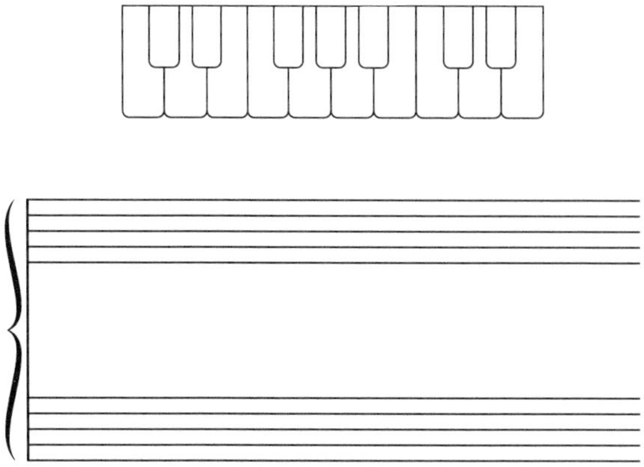

g. F♯ harmonic minor

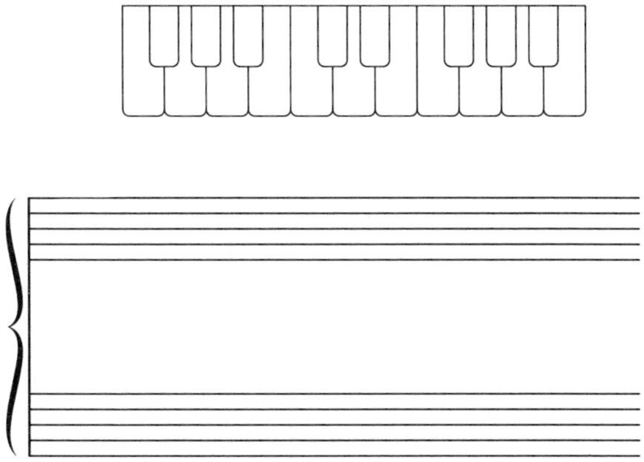

h. B♭ harmonic minor

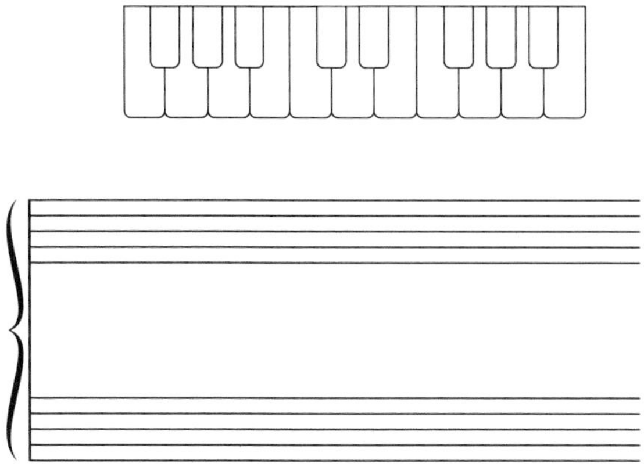

i. C♯ harmonic minor

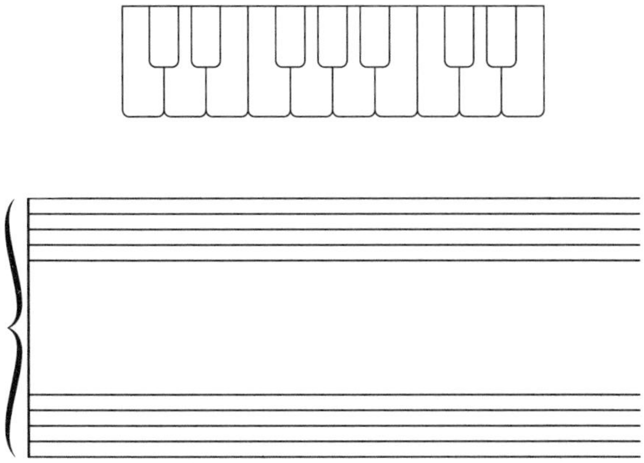

j. E♭ harmonic minor

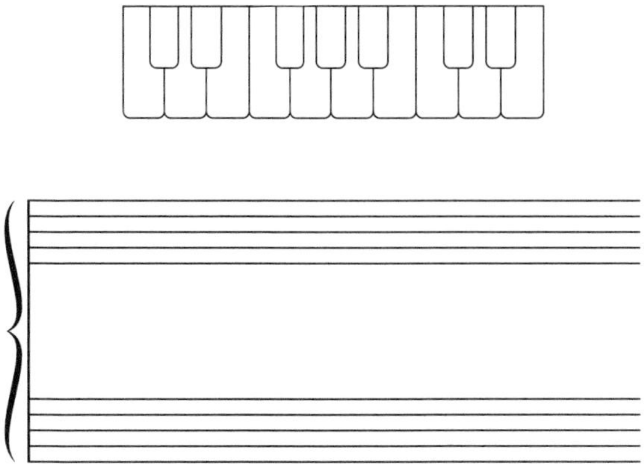

Other harmonic minor scales appear in Appendix II, pp. 238–39.

The Melodic Minor Scale

The **melodic minor scale** differs from the other minor scales because it ascends using one set of pitches (one pattern of whole and half steps) and descends using another. In the melodic minor scale, both the 6th and 7th scale degrees are raised a half step when ascending; they are then lowered a half step when descending, restoring them to their natural positions. On the keyboard and staff, the melodic minor looks like this:

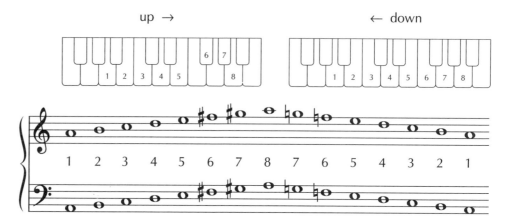

Like the other forms of the minor scale, the melodic minor evolved from musical usage. Composers who used them *sometimes* heard the raised 6th and 7th degrees pushing toward the tonic going up, and the lowered 6th and 7th degrees pushing toward the 5th scale degree going down. (In Chapter Eight, we will see the importance of the 5th scale degree in tonal music.) Note the melodic minor scale in the following excerpt:

Bourrée   J. S. Bach

12 Write the following melodic minor scales on each staff of the grand staff. Use the scale given above as an example. Be sure to include the appropriate clefs and key signatures.

a. C melodic minor

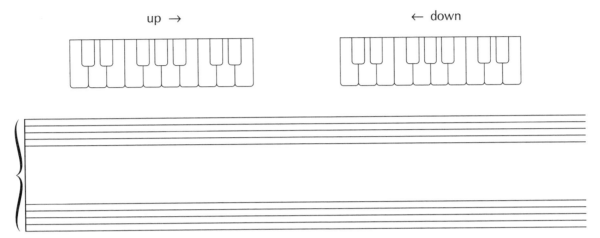

b. D melodic minor

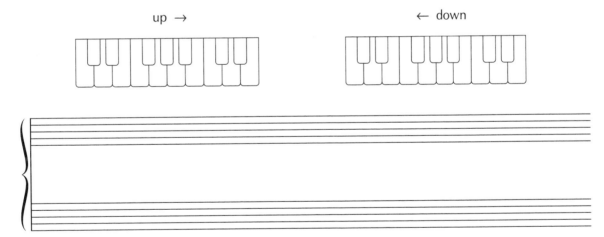

c. B melodic minor

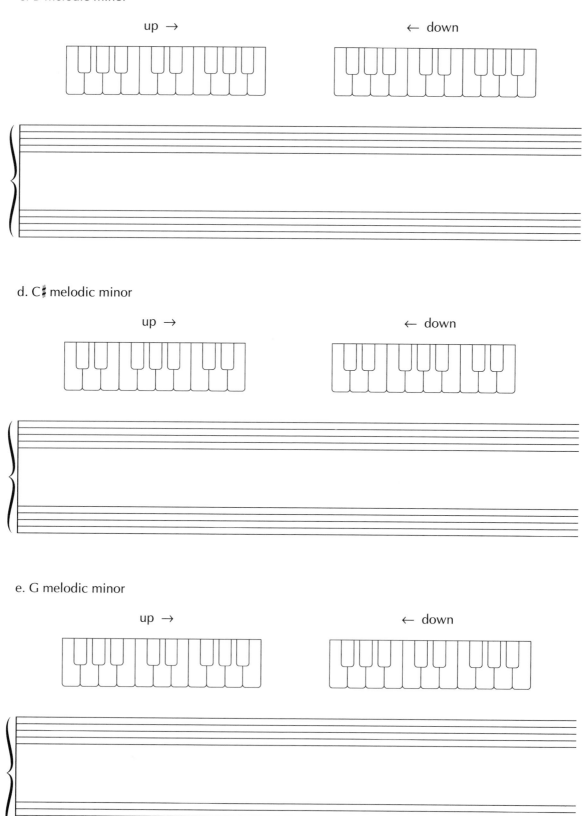

d. C♯ melodic minor

e. G melodic minor

f. F melodic minor

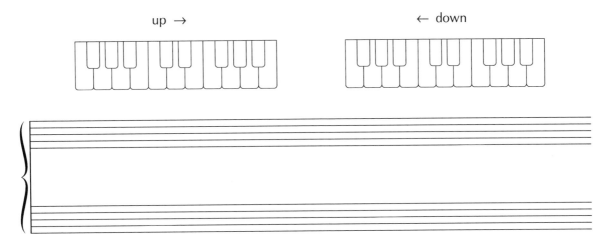

Minor Scales and Musical Usage

Scales are a theoretical concept. Thinking that composers always used them as strict forms would be a mistake. Most often in pieces of music, we find a mixture of several scales, sometimes used in nonconventional ways. For example, in the following pieces, the raised 6th and 7th degrees of the melodic minor scale are heard both ascending and descending:

1. Chorale Melody (from *Cantata No. 198*)   J. S. Bach

Key: B minor

2. *Kyrie* (adapted)   Mozart

Key: D minor

3. *Air* (from *Suite III*)   Handel

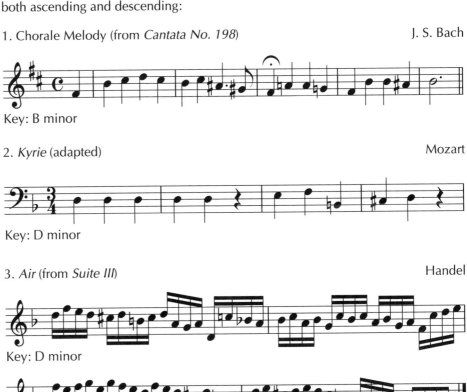

Key: D minor

The Chromatic Scale

One other type of scale featured in many musical compositions is the **chromatic scale**. This scale is built solely of ascending and descending half steps and uses all twelve tones of the octave on the piano keyboard. It is therefore not a diatonic scale, because most of the pitch names repeat but with chromatic alterations. Note that when ascending, the chromatic pitches are notated with sharps, and when descending, they are notated with flats.

ASCENDING CHROMATIC SCALE USING SHARPS

DESCENDING CHROMATIC SCALE USING FLATS

Notice that each letter name is used twice in the ascending scale *except* for E and B, because a half step above each of these notes is the adjacent white key with a different letter name. Similarly, in the descending chromatic scale, C and F are written only once, because a half step below each of these notes is the adjacent white key.

13 Finish numbering this ascending chromatic scale, which starts on A, and notate it below. Then play and name the notes.

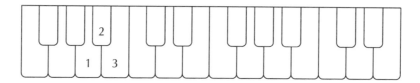

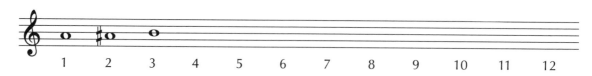

14 Finish numbering this descending chromatic scale, which starts on F, and notate it below. Play and name the notes.

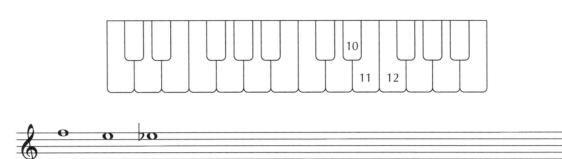

12 11 10 9 8 7 6 5 4 3 2 1

TERMS, SYMBOLS, AND CONCEPTS

natural minor scale   chromatic scale
relative minor   leading tone
relative minor key signature   harmonic minor
relative major key signature   melodic minor
parallel major and minor   chromatic scale

SUGGESTED ACTIVITIES

1. Transpose the following natural minor melodies:

    Dear Willie (*Scorebook* 30) to E minor

    The Welcome Song (*Scorebook* 46) to B minor

2. Choose from among the following melodies and examine them for treatment of the 7th degree of the minor scale:

    Melody (Finnish) (*Scorebook* 14)

    Que ne suis-je la fougère (*Scorebook* 15)

    Jeune fillette (*Scorebook* 16)

    The Hunter (*Scorebook* 18)

Carraig Aonair (*Scorebook* 19)

The Knife Sharpener (*Scorebook* 21)

La paloma (*Scorebook* 36)

Christmas Has Come (*Scorebook* 51)

Bach, *Puer natus in Bethlehem* (*Scorebook* 57)

3. Choose from among the following pieces and examine them for use of natural, harmonic, or melodic minor scales:

Willie, Take Your Little Drum (*Scorebook* 50)

Ringing of the Bells (*Scorebook* 53)

Turn Me 'Round (*Scorebook* 54)

Bach, Chorale Melody from *The Wedding Cantata* (*Scorebook* 58)

Handel, Theme from *Concerto Grosso No. 5* (*Scorebook* 66)

4. Examine all scale types and parallel major and minor scales in *Planting Song* (*Scorebook* 49).

5. Compose a melody containing two or more phrases in the natural minor scale.

6. Compose a melody containing two or more phrases that combines various forms of the minor scale.

CHAPTER EIGHT

Harmony and Chords

The simultaneous sounding of more than one pitch is called **harmony**. In Chapter Four, we learned that when two pitches sound at the same time, a harmonic interval is created. When three or more pitches sound together, we have a **chord**. In tonal music, chords are the building blocks of harmony. Note the following examples of chords.

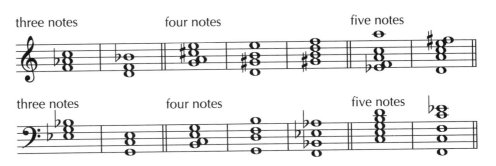

Triads

A **triad** is a three-note chord formed by two intervals of a 3rd. The lowest note of a triad is called the **root**, the middle note the **3rd**, and the top note the **5th**. This terminology reflects the intervallic relationship of the upper two notes to the root. The root gives the triad its letter name. Triads are the most common type of chords used in tonal harmony. Study these triads.

1 Construct triads on each of the specified notes. If the root of a triad is on a space, all the notes will be on consecutive spaces. If the root is on a line, all the notes will also be on lines. Label each triad with R, 3, and 5 (representing the root, 3rd, and 5th). Name the root. Use no sharps or flats.

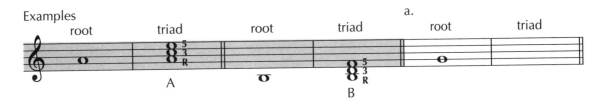

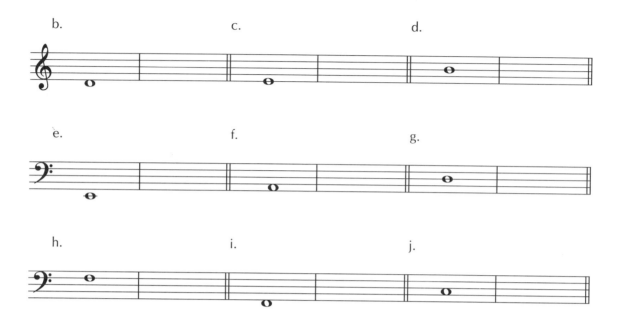

Quality of Triads

Like intervals, triads may differ in quality. A triad's quality depends on the quality of the intervals it contains. The two basic types of triads, the major triad and the minor triad, differ in quality in the following way: the **major triad** contains a M3 and a P5 above the root, and the **minor triad** contains a m3 and a P5 above the root.

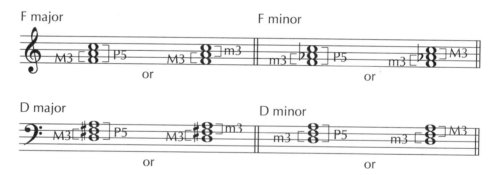

Triads and Scales

We can use major and minor scales as a model for spelling major and minor triads. The intervals of a major triad correspond to the tonic, 3rd, and 5th degrees of the major scale, while the intervals of a minor triad correspond to the tonic, 3rd, and 5th degrees of the minor scale. Comparing the first five notes of any parallel major and minor scale, we find that the only note they don't share is the 3rd. The same holds true for any major and minor triads built on the same note. Both contain a P5 between the root and the 5th, but each has a different 3rd between the root and the 3rd. This difference in the quality of the 3rd is easy to remember: the major scale and major triad contain a *major 3rd* (M3) between 1 and 3; the minor scale and minor triad, a *minor 3rd* (m3).

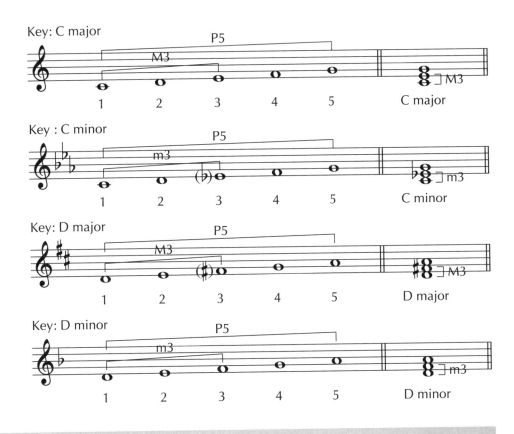

2   Write the indicated key signature, then write the first five notes of each scale. Finally, write the triad that corresponds to the scale tones. Study the example carefully.

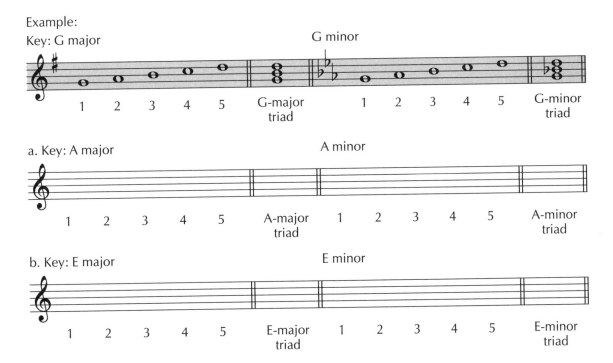

c. Key: B♭ major   B♭ minor

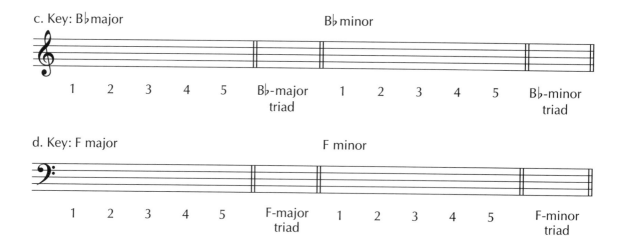

1   2   3   4   5   B♭-major   1   2   3   4   5   B♭-minor
                          triad   triad

d. Key: F major   F minor

1   2   3   4   5   F-major   1   2   3   4   5   F-minor
                          triad   triad

3   Change each of these major triads to a minor triad by *lowering* the 3rd a half step. This alteration can be accomplished by adding an accidental to the 3rd or by changing the accidental already there. The letter name spelling must remain the same. To lower a natural note (white key), use a flat; to lower a sharp note, use a natural sign. Indicate both the chords that are given and the new chords on the keyboard diagrams.

Examples:

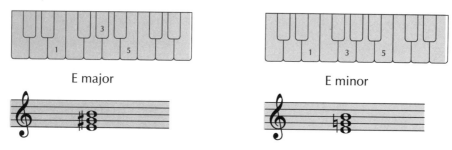

E major   E minor

The natural sign is used here to lower G♯ to G♮.

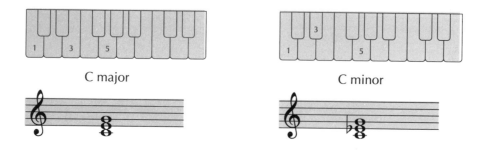

C major   C minor

The flat sign is used here to lower E to E♭.

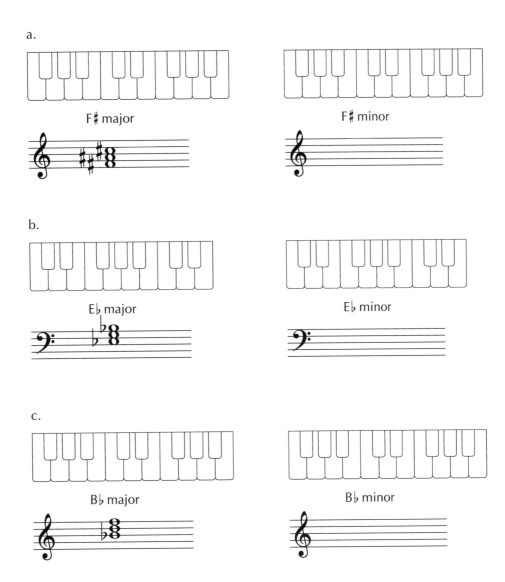

a.

F♯ major

F♯ minor

b.

E♭ major

E♭ minor

c.

B♭ major

B♭ minor

4 Change each of these minor triads to a major triad by *raising* the 3rd a half step. To raise a natural note, use a sharp. To raise a flat note, use a natural sign. Indicate both the chords that are given and the new chords on the keyboard diagrams.

Examples:

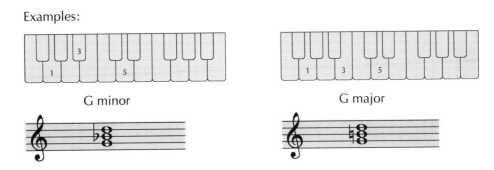

G minor

G major

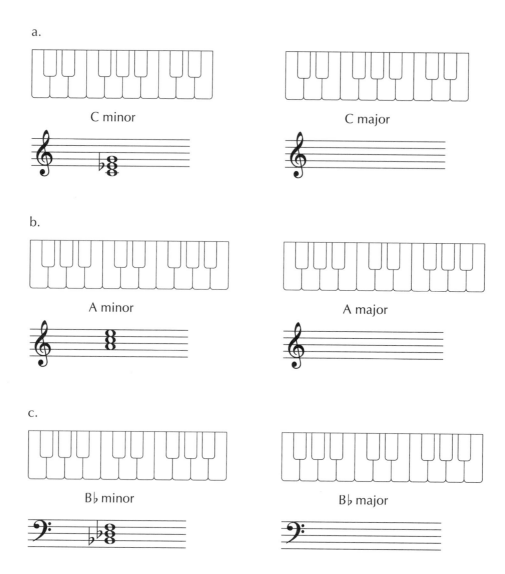

a.

C minor   C major

b.

A minor   A major

c.

B♭ minor   B♭ major

Working with Triads

The only way to learn triads thoroughly is to work with them. To this end, your objectives will be:

1. to learn three groups of triads outlined below *note perfect*;
2. to hear triads as building blocks in tonal harmony;
3. to hear the triadic background of many melodies.

Some of the examples in this chapter have no key signatures because you will learn to spell triads more quickly if you always write the necessary accidentals. Think of triads as new words in the musical language you are learning. In that light, the exercises that follow can be thought of as conversational practice.

Here we will start using an abbreviated way of labeling triads: a capital letter to indicate major triads, and a capital letter plus a small m to indicate minor triads. Thus, C major, D major, and A major become C, D, and A; and C minor, D minor, and A minor become Cm, Dm, and Am.

Learning the Triads   As a temporary learning aid, we will arrange triads into three separate groups. These groups have no theoretical significance but rather are simply a method for remembering triad spelling. They ultimately will help to distinguish triads built on any pitch. This temporary system gives us a vocabulary of chords we can use immediately.

GROUP I: MAJOR AND MINOR TRIADS ON G, C, AND F

Major triads with no accidentals fall on the notes G, C, and F. To form a minor triad from a major triad that has no accidentals, simply add a flat to the 3rd.

GROUP II: MAJOR AND MINOR TRIADS ON E, A, AND D

Major triads with a sharp on the third fall on the notes E, A, and D. To form a minor triad from a major triad that has a sharp on the third, simply omit the sharp, or change it to a natural sign.

5   Play and name aloud each triad. Do not write their names in the book.

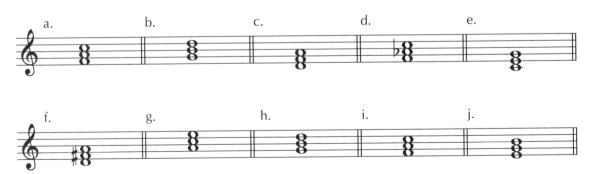

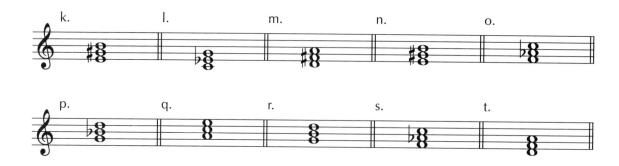

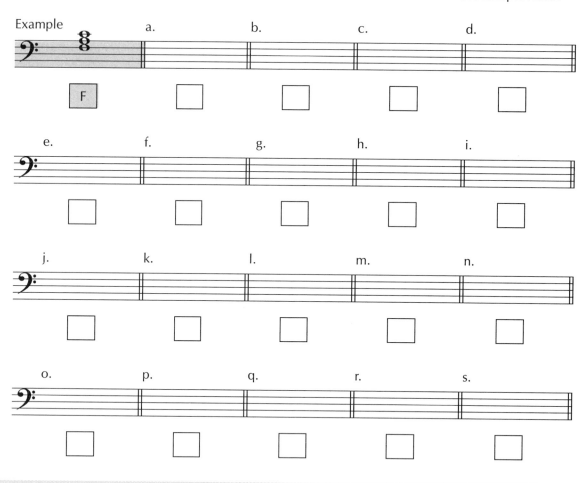

6 Write each of the triads found in exercise #5 in the bass clef. Name each one in the box provided.

Triads on B and B♭ All the triads studied thus far contain a natural perfect 5th (both the root and the 5th of these chords are white keys). There are two instances, however, where only the root *or* the 5th is on a white key: these are the triads built on B and B♭. When we construct a major or minor triad on the note B, we need an F♯ to create a perfect 5th. Similarly, when the note F is the 5th of a major or minor triad, its root must be B♭ (see also Chapter 6, page 96). The triads built on B and B♭, therefore, form a special case and should be studied as a separate group:

GROUP III: TRIADS ON B AND B♭

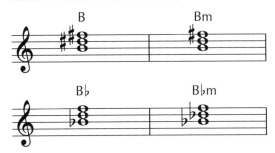

7   Write the following triads.

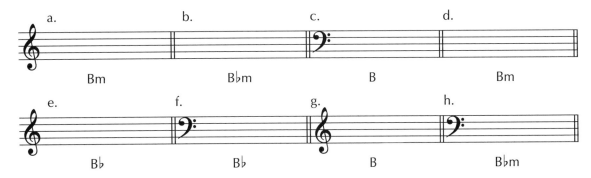

8   Name the following triads as quickly as you can. Record your fastest time in the space provided below. Use the additional space that is provided for future timings.

Time

Voicing

We have been studying triads in their simplest form, with the root as the lowest note and the 3rd and the 5th directly above it. In actual use, the root, 3rd, or 5th may appear in different octaves and in different combinations. Such positioning of the pitches of a triad is called **voicing**. The following example shows different voicings of the Gm triad. If a pitch appears more than once, we say it is **doubled**. No matter how complicated these different chords may seem, they all use only the root, 3rd, and 5th of the Gm triad.

BASIC TRIAD

DIFFERENT VOICINGS

Voicing for Four-Part Chorus

The following chords demonstrate several voicings of a Gm triad for four-part chorus (soprano, alto, tenor, and bass). With four parts and only three notes to work with, doubling becomes necessary. Each voicing has its own characteristic sound, which can be heard by playing the examples on the keyboard or singing the four-part harmony with your colleagues.

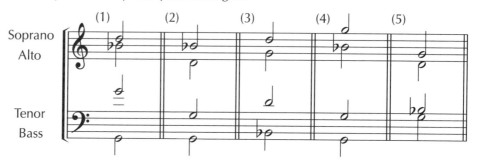

Note that the chord in example (4) leaves out one note of the triad (D).

---

9   Rewrite each chord in its simplest triadic form in both clefs. Name the triad in the box provided, then label each note in the given triad as root (R), 3rd (3), or 5th (5).

Example:

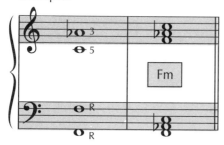

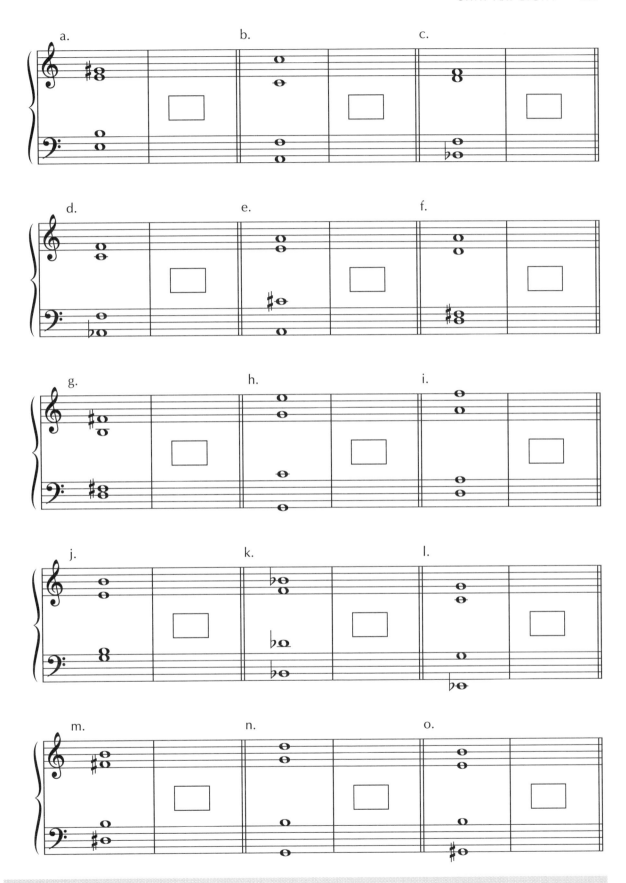

Chord Inversions   When the lowest note of a triad voicing is the root, we say that the triad is in **root position**. When the lowest note of a triad is *not* the root, the triad is said to be **inverted**. There are two ways in which a triad appears in inversion: when the 3rd of the triad is the lowest note, and when the 5th is the lowest note. With the 3rd as the lowest note, the triad is in **first inversion**. With the 5th as the lowest note, the triad is in **second inversion**. Notice that this use of inversion, similar to intervallic inversion (see p. 60), involves changes in pitch to a different octave.

INVERSIONS OF A TRIAD

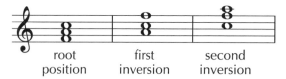

root position   first inversion   second inversion

10   Write the first and second inversions of these triads. Name each triad. Study the example.

Example:

Harmonic Background of a Melody

Sometimes the intervals in a melody outline a triad, providing a clear example of the melody's **harmonic background**. We can define harmonic background as the chord pattern that fits the tune. In folk and popular music, the harmonic background is usually indicated by the chord names that appear above the melody. While these designations do not appear in classical music, we can add them in when we analyze the music. The following melodies indicate their harmonic backgrounds, easily identified by the outline of particular triads:

a. *Black, Black, Black*   Traditional

1. Black, black, black is the col-or of my true love's hair;

b. *Prelude*   J. S. Bach

---

11   In the following excerpts, write the names of the bracketed triads. Consider all the notes in both clefs.

a. *Minuet* (*Scorebook* 73)   Mozart

b. *Gigue*   J. S. Bach

Harmonic Progression

The succession of chords in a musical composition is called a **harmonic progression**, often shortened to "chord progression" (or just "progression"). For example, when describing the first phrase from *Black, Black, Black* on the previous page, we can say, "the progression is from D minor to A minor."

Composing a Chord Melody

To develop facility with triads, we will now compose some melodies that consist only of the pitches in a succession of triads. The examples below demonstrate how to use the harmonic progressions and rhythms to compose a simple chord melody. Notice that you may choose any combination of the triad's tones. You may even repeat a pitch of the triad in a measure. Although the key is indicated, these exercises do not show key signatures. Writing every accidental will help you learn the correct spelling of each triad.

Example:

12 Compose melodies to these four-measure chord progressions. Use only tones from the indicated chord. If more than one chord appears in a measure, use the pitches of the first chord until the next chord starts. For example:

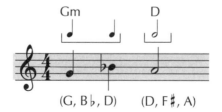

Now rewrite the second melody (b) using the key signature of G minor.

Rewrite the third melody (c) using the key signature of C minor.

d. Make up your own rhythm. Use an A-major key signature:

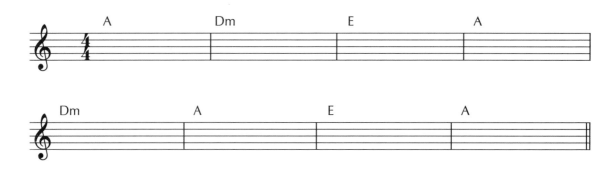

e. Make up your own rhythm. Use a B-minor key signature:

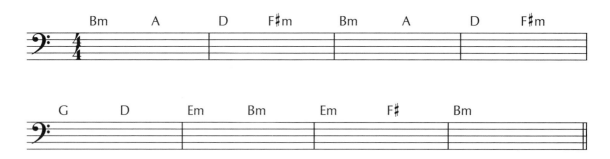

Nonchord Tones

Melodies consisting exclusively of chord tones are rare. While a melody may have a distinct harmonic background in which chord tones play a vital role, many pitches will not fit the specific chord of the harmonic background. These notes are called **nonchord** (or sometimes **nonharmonic**) **tones**. This terminology does not imply that these tones don't sound good. Quite the contrary. The interplay between chord tones and nonchord tones is an essential feature of tonal music. The following examples demonstrate some of the ways nonchord tones relate to the harmonic background.

Neighbor Tones

Earlier we saw that the opening phrase of *Black, Black, Black* outlined a D-minor triad. Two nonchord tones are also present: the G in measure 1 and the C in measure 2 (circled below). Each is considered a **neighbor tone** because it moves stepwise from a chord tone but immediately returns to it. In this example, both neighbor tones fall *below* the chord tones. We refer to these tones as **lower neighbors**.

In measure 1 of Purcell's *Minuet*, we find neighbor tones both *below* and *above* the chord tone. Notice that the G♯, the lower neighbor, is a chromatic note. Chromatic accidentals appear often as nonchord tones. The B above the chord tone is called an **upper neighbor**.

Minuet (*Scorebook* 63)   Purcell

Passing Tones

Another type of nonchord tone is called the **passing tone**. Passing tones occur when the melodic line *passes* through a note in stepwise motion to get from one chord tone to another. In the example below, the harmony in measure 1 is G minor, making the G and B♭ chord tones. Notice how the melody passes from G to B♭ through the pitch A. This note, which is circled, is therefore a passing tone. Passing tones also occur in measures 2, 3, and 4. Compare the notes that are circled in these measures with the harmonies that are indicated above the staff:

La paloma (*Scorebook* 36)   Spanish

In measure 2 of the next example, the harmony is G. Notice how passing tones move stepwise from one chord to another in three of the four voices:

Chorale from *Cantata No. 43* (*Scorebook* 79)   J. S. Bach

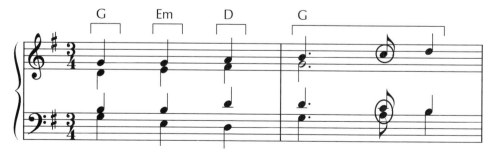

Other nonchord tones are often heard in scale passages, or sections of music drawn from the scale on which the section or piece is based. In the following excerpt, the nonchord tones are pitches from the G-minor scale:

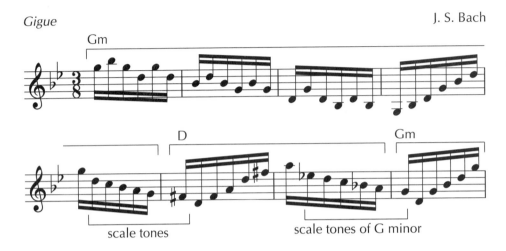

13 Circle all the nonchord tones in the following examples.

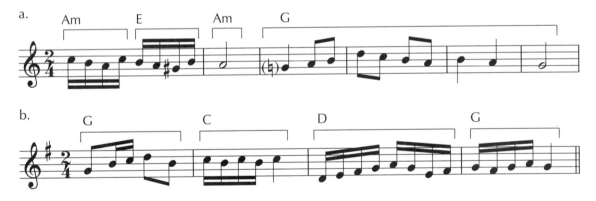

Notating Voices: Various Methods

There are various ways to notate separate voices. One is to write a separate staff for each voice, as demonstrated in *Ringing of the Bells* (*Scorebook* 53) and *Remember, O Thou Man* (*Scorebook* 77).

Other methods are more flexible. For instance, in *All the Stars* (*Scorebook* 52), all the voices are put on the same staff—the upper voice with note stems up, the lower two voices with note stems down—although the harmonies change from three to two voices. By contrast, in *Turn Me 'Round* (*Scorebook* 54), the harmonies are presented with a more informal type of stemming to encourage improvisation. Here, the performers sing the melody, then just pick any note of the harmony on the words "turn me 'round." In the second part of the song, on the words "keep on a-walking," the parts split in two; the lower part features a constant D that finally rises to the tonic, G.

Harmonizing a Melody with 3rds and 6ths

Many traditional melodies can be harmonized by using either 3rds or 6ths. The following version of *The First Noel* demonstrates this practice. Notice how the two parts have their own note stems, the higher part with stems going up and the lower part with stems going down. This is true even when both parts sing in unison, on a note that has two stems attached to it. This example begins in unison, and then the parts separate, forming 3rds and 6ths.

The First Noel   Traditional

14 Write a harmony for each of these melodies using 3rds or 6ths.

Example:

melody

harmony

a. Use 6ths:

melody

harmony

b. Use 3rds:

harmony

melody

c. Use 3rds and 6ths:

melody

harmony

Canons and Rounds

An interesting type of piece in which parts can produce harmony is the **canon**, or **round**. A canon is a piece in which two or more voices perform the same melody at different times. A round is the popular name for a canon. These pieces may often continue indefinitely as each voice part repeats itself.

15 Sing the following canons and rounds from the *Scorebook*:

Dona nobis pacem (*Scorebook* 43)

Hey, Ho, Nobody at Home (*Scorebook* 45)

The Welcome Song (*Scorebook* 46)

Oh How Lovely Is the Evening (*Scorebook* 44)

The Blue Note Canon (*Scorebook* 48)

TERMS, SYMBOLS, AND CONCEPTS

chord

triad

major triad

minor triad

relationship between major scale
    and triad

relationship between minor scale
    and triad

chord voicing

root position of a triad

first inversion

second inversion

harmonic background

harmonic progression

chord tone

nonchord tone

soprano

alto

tenor

bass

notating voices on the staff

canon

round

SUGGESTED ACTIVITIES

1. Name the notes of the following triads from memory: C, Cm, D, Dm, E, Em, F, Fm, G, Gm, A, Am, B♭, B♭m, B, Bm.

2. Compose a melody using one of the progressions from numbers 1–4 in Appendix V.

3. Compose a chord melody to your own progression.

4. Bracket and name any triads (in various positions and patterns) you find in the following melodies in the *Scorebook*:

   Believe Me if All Those Endearing Young Charms (*Scorebook* 42)

   Mozart, *Minuet* (*Scorebook* 73) (except for those measures with boxes)

5. Examine the following melodies for harmony and nonchord tones. Bracket any clearly outlined triads. Compare all notes with the harmony written above them. If any don't fit the chord, circle them as nonchord tones:

Barbrie Allen (*Scorebook* 27)

The Trees They Do Grow High (*Scorebook* 29)

Dear Willie (*Scorebook* 30)

Johnny Has Gone for a Soldier (*Scorebook* 34)

En el portal de Belén (*Scorebook* 37)

CHAPTER NINE

Complex Triad Spellings

Spelling some triads can look complicated when numerous accidentals, including double sharps and double flats, are necessary. No matter how complex the accidentals used, however, the letter-name spelling must always remain the same. For instance, any triad built on a G, G♯, or G♭ will show the same basic letter-name spelling: G-B-D. Always remember the basic letter-name spellings when notating triads. Observe the spelling of the following:

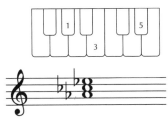

A♭ minor

Notice that since the basic letter-name spelling is A-C-E, the 3rd must be spelled C♭, *not B♮*.

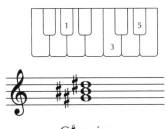

G♯ major

Notice that since the basic letter-name spelling is G-B-D, the 3rd must be spelled B♯, *not C*.

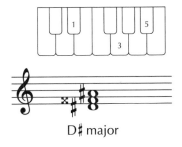

D♯ major

Since the basic letter-name spelling is D-F-A, the 3rd must be spelled F double sharp (F𝄪), *not G*.

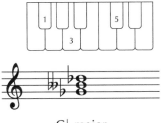

G♭ major

Since the basic letter-name spelling is G-B-D, the 3rd must be spelled B double flat (B♭♭), *not A*.

An Aid for Spelling Other Triads

In Chapter Eight, we learned to spell all triads on the white keys. The spelling of white-key triads can be used to find the correct spelling of other triads:

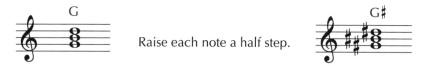

In the example above, since each note of the G♯ triad has been raised a half step, the same interval relationship is maintained. The G triad becomes the G♯ triad. The same process applies to the minor triad on G:

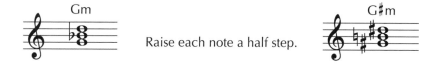

In the example above, notice that you must use a natural sign in order to raise B♭ a half step. Whether to use a sharp, flat, or natural is determined by the note's function. The process of altering the tones of a triad while maintaining their function will often involve a combination of various accidentals. Sharps and flats, however, *never appear together* when spelling any major or minor triad.

---

1 Play the following triads. Observe how the more complex spellings are derived by raising or lowering a triad by a half step.

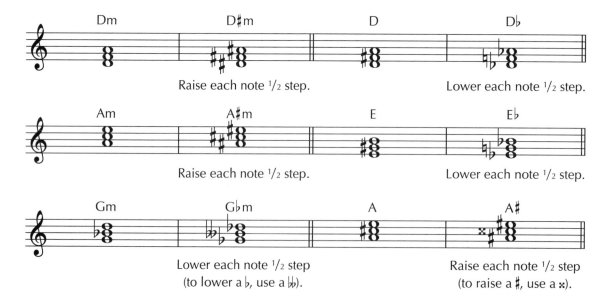

2 Complete the following sentences. Review the use of accidentals, if necessary.

   a. If you raise all the notes of a triad one half step, the new triad will have (the same, a different)

   _____ quality.

   b. To raise a flat one half step, you use a _____.

   c. To lower a sharp one half step, you use a _____.

   d. To lower a flat one half step, you use a _____.

   e. To raise a sharp one half step, you use a _____.

3 Raise or lower each of the following triads a half step. Be careful to use the correct accidentals. Name each triad. Study the example carefully.

Example:

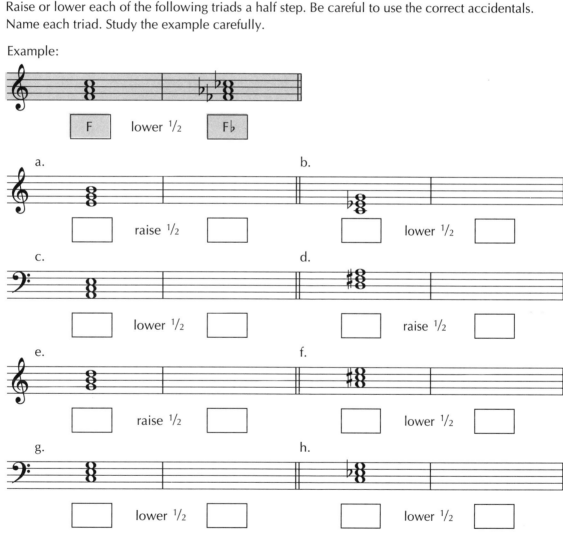

Diminished and Augmented Triads

In addition to major and minor, triads may be diminished or augmented. The **diminished triad** (dim or °) contains a minor 3rd and a diminished 5th above the root. It can also be thought of as two minor 3rds.

DIMINISHED TRIAD

The **augmented triad** (aug) is built with a major 3rd and an augmented 5th above the root. It can also be thought of as two major 3rds.

AUGMENTED TRIAD

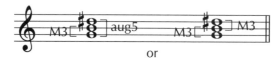

Altering Triads

On page 130, we changed a major triad to a minor triad by altering the third. This method for learning triads can be extended to diminished and augmented triads. By spelling each of the four types of triads on the same note, you will quickly learn the triads and grasp the intervallic relationships among them.

To change a *major* triad to a *minor* triad, *lower* the 3rd a half step.

To change a *minor* triad to a *diminished* triad, *lower* the 5th a half step.

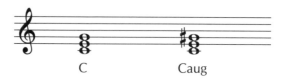

To change a *major* triad to an *augmented* triad, *raise* the 5th a half step.

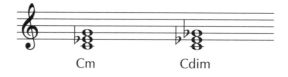

4 Using the procedures described above, write major, minor, diminished, and augmented triads on the indicated pitches.

Example:

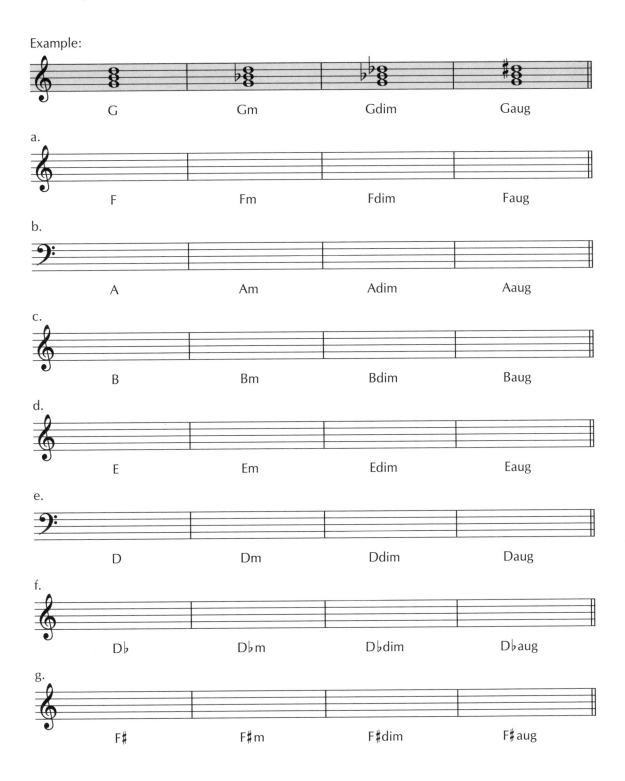

G   Gm   Gdim   Gaug

a.

F   Fm   Fdim   Faug

b.

A   Am   Adim   Aaug

c.

B   Bm   Bdim   Baug

d.

E   Em   Edim   Eaug

e.

D   Dm   Ddim   Daug

f.

D♭   D♭m   D♭dim   D♭aug

g.

F♯   F♯m   F♯dim   F♯aug

h.

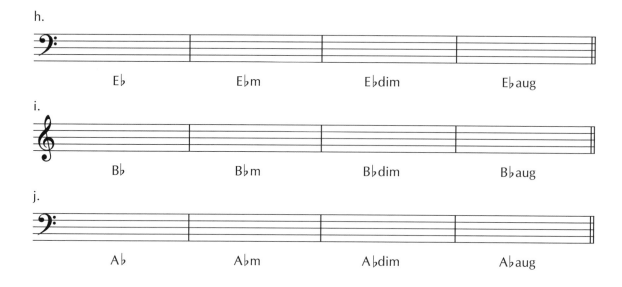

Eb   Ebm   Ebdim   Ebaug

i.

Bb   Bbm   Bbdim   Bbaug

j.

Ab   Abm   Abdim   Abaug

TRIAD QUALITY

Ascending, from root to 3rd to 5th:

A **major** triad contains a *major* 3rd and a perfect 5th.

A **minor** triad contains a *minor* 3rd and a perfect 5th.

A **diminished** triad contains a minor 3rd and a *diminished* 5th.

An **augmented** triad contains a major 3rd and an *augmented* 5th.

Notice which interval names the triad.

The Harmonic System

We have focused our study of harmony so far on the root and quality of triads. We will now examine the **harmonic system**, or how triads relate to each other within a key. Let's start by building triads on each scale degree, using only tones from the scale. Observe the quality of each triad.

Key: C major

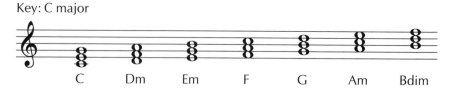

C   Dm   Em   F   G   Am   Bdim

We can give each triad a Roman numeral designation that represents the triad's *position in the key*. Major triads are designated with large Roman numerals (I, IV, V), and minor triads with small Roman numerals (ii, iii, vi). Note that the one diminished triad, built on the 7th scale degree, is identified by a small Roman numeral followed by a diminished symbol, ° (vii°).

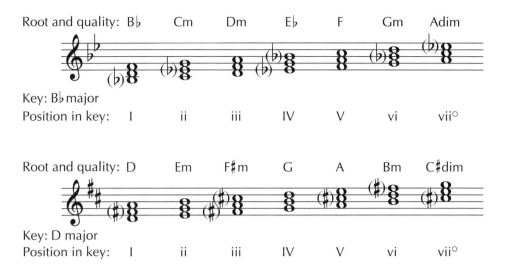

Root and quality: B♭   Cm   Dm   E♭   F   Gm   Adim

Key: B♭ major
Position in key: I   ii   iii   IV   V   vi   vii°

Root and quality: D   Em   F♯m   G   A   Bm   C♯dim

Key: D major
Position in key: I   ii   iii   IV   V   vi   vii°

5 Repeat the procedure outlined above for the following keys. Write the key signatures first. Place parentheses around any accidentals from the key signature when they appear in a chord. The quality of each chord (indicated by a large or small Roman numeral) will be the same in every major key when using only scale tones to build the triad. You are merely transposing relationships unchanged from one key to another. Name the root and quality as above.

a. Root and quality:

Key: E♭ major
Position in key: I   ii   iii   IV   V   vi   vii°

b. Root and quality:

Key: F major
Position in key: I   ii   iii   IV   V   vi   vii°

c. Root and quality:

Key: G major
Position in key: I   ii   iii   IV   V   vi   vii°

d. Root and quality:

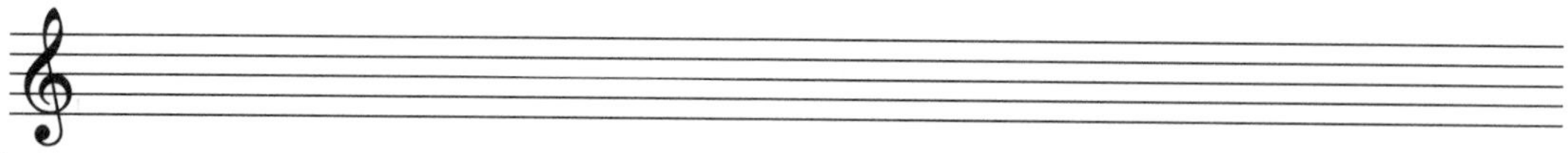

Key: B♭ major

Position in key: I   ii   iii   IV   V   vi   vii°

e. Root and quality:

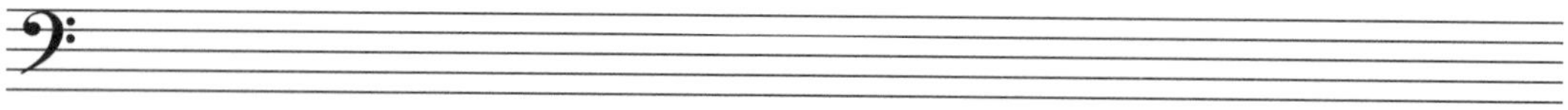

Key: A major

Position in key: I   ii   iii   IV   V   vi   vii°

f. Root and quality:

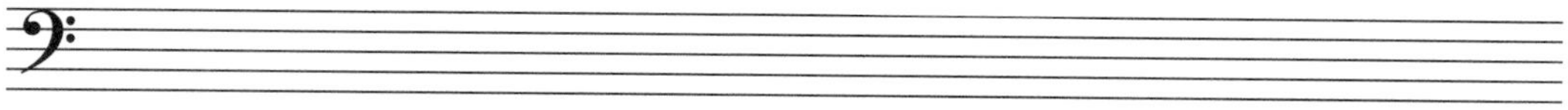

Key: A♭ major

Position in key: I   ii   iii   IV   V   vi   vii°

g. Root and quality:

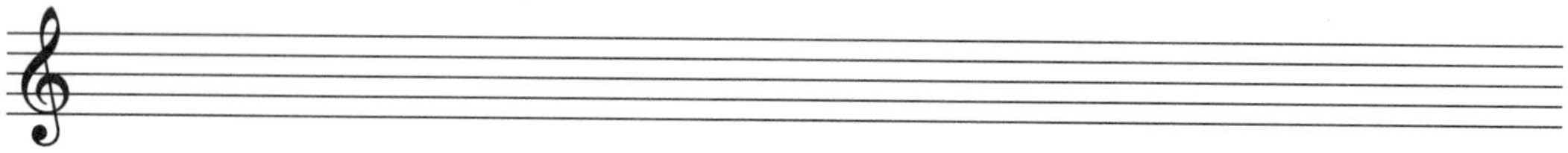

Key: E major

Position in key: I   ii   iii   IV   V   vi   vii°

h. Root and quality:

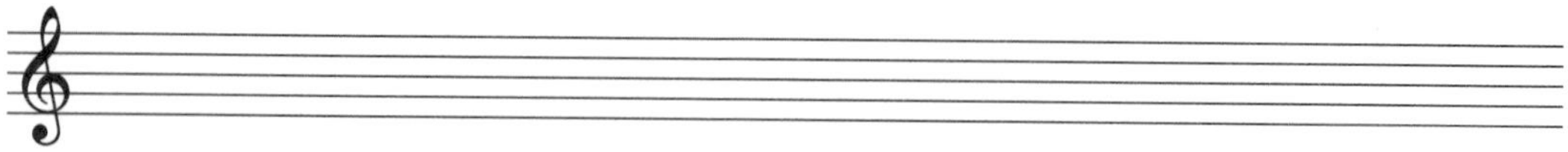

Key: B major

Position in key: I   ii   iii   IV   V   vi   vii°

MAJOR-SCALE TRIAD QUALITY

The I chord is major.   The V chord is major.
The ii chord is minor.   The vi chord is minor.
The iii chord is minor.   The vii° chord is diminished.
The IV chord is major.

---

6   Complete the following sentences by writing the root and quality of the required triad.

If only scale tones have been used to build the chord:

Ex. The iii chord in the key of C major is _____Em_____.

a. The ii chord in the key of B♭ major is _____.

b. The iii chord in the key of D major is _____.

c. The IV chord in the key of A major is _____.

d. The IV chord in the key of B major is _____.

e. The V chord in the key of B♭ major is _____.

f.   The vi chord in the key of E major is _____.

g. The vii° chord in the key of C major is _____.

h. The V chord in F♯ major is _____.

i.   The iii chord in E major is _____.

j.   The IV chord in E♭ major is _____.

7   In each of the following exercises, write the required triad. Name the root and quality of each triad.

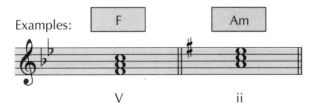

Examples: F   Am

V   ii

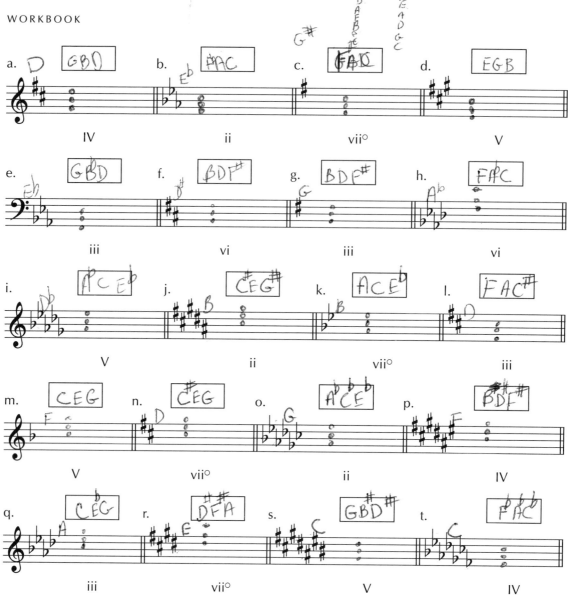

8 Analyze the first phrase of Schütz's *Psalm 75* for triad quality and position in key. (This excerpt begins with an exception to the major-scale triad quality rule: a minor chord on the fifth scale degree. It is therefore indicated with the symbol "v." Remember that the accidental applies to the first measure only.) Notice that the last chord has no third.

Psalm 75 (Scorebook 77)   Heinrich Schütz

Transposing Chords

Naming chords within a key is important for understanding harmonic movement, or, as we have called it, the chord progression. As a practical demonstration of the harmonic system, imagine a performer **transposing** a song from one key to another. The first phrase of the song looks like this:

Barbrie Allen (Scorebook 27)

The performer wishes to play the song in a higher key—let's say Eb, F, or G. What chords will be correct in the new keys? The performer who is familiar with the harmonic system can think of how the chords relate to one another:

Chords in original key:	D	G	D	A	D	A	D	Bm	F#m
Position in key:	I	IV	I	V	I	V	I	vi	iii
Chord in other keys:	Eb	Ab	Eb	Bb	Eb	Bb	Eb	Cm	Gm
	F	Bb	F	C	F	C	F	Dm	Am
	G	C	G	D	G	D	G	Em	Bm

9 Refer to *Barbrie Allen (Scorebook 27)* for the following two exercises.

a. In the blanks provided, label the chords of the second phrase.

Phrase I

Chords:	D	G	D	A	D	A	D	Bm	F#m
Position in key:	I	IV	I	V	I	V	I	vi	iii

Phrase II

Chords:	G	D	A	Bm	A	D	G	A	D
Position in key:	___	___	___	___	___	___	___	___	___

b. Transpose the complete song to E major. Write the names of the chords above the staff. Write the Roman numerals of the "position in key" below it.

Motive

Many melodies and musical compositions are based on short, recurring ideas called **motives**. A motive functions as a unifying element in music, helping to organize rhythm, melody, and form. Composers use motives in very creative and flexible ways. A motive can be just a few notes in length or contain just one rhythmic pattern. But when repeated or altered, the motive can take on great significance and help to shape an entire melody and even a complete piece of music.

Rhythmic Identity of a Motive

A motive sometimes presents a specific rhythmic idea, which underlies the rhythmic structure of a melody when the motive is repeated several times. Consider the following melody, consisting of a seven-note motive that is repeated four times:

Theme from *Don Giovanni* (*Scorebook* 60)   Mozart

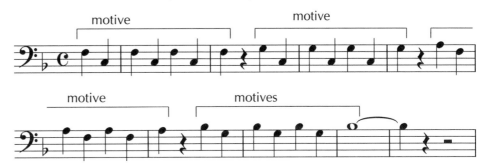

The motive's seven notes alternate between two pitches (F and C) that form the interval of a perfect 4th. When this motive is repeated, the interval changes—first to a perfect 5th (G and C), then to a major 3rd (A and F), and last to a minor 3rd (B♭ and G)—before the seven-note pattern changes on the tied whole note, B♭. This last note, B♭, halts the rhythmic repetition of the motive and signifies the cadence that ends the first phrase.

Pitch Identity of a Motive

A motive has a definite pitch design. Consider the following melody in D minor:

The Hunter (*Scorebook* 18)

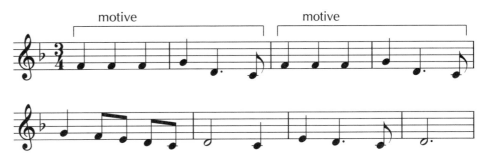

We can immediately recognize the motive in this melody because it *repeats* in measures 3 and 4. But how does the motive appear in the last four measures of the phrase? At first glance, these measures seem quite different from the first four. But a closer look at the pitches in measures 5–8 reveals that the musical phrase has grown out of the original motive:

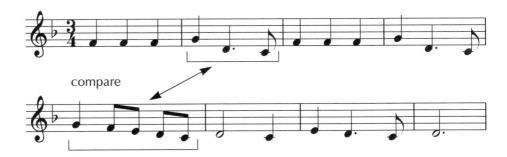

Note that the pitches of measure 2 span a 4th and a 2nd, from G to D and then D to C. If we compare measure 2 with measure 5, we find the same span of pitches, but filled in with the remaining scale steps, on pitches F and E. (In these two measures the first and last notes are the same: G and C.) Thus, the portion of the original motive in measure 2 has been expanded in measure 5.

An even smaller part of the original motive is repeated throughout the melody, especially in the remaining measures:

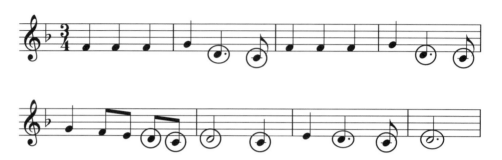

Because they repeat again and again, the pitches D and C (circled above) become a prominent part of the musical phrase. Since D is the tonic, this repetition is all the more important. This motive has a strong **pitch identity**, consisting of the notes F, G, D, and C. An important part of this motive's pitch identity is the relationship between the last two pitches, D and C.

Sequence

A motive can reappear transformed in a melody in various ways. Two that we will learn here are sequence and inversion. A **sequence** is an immediate repetition of a motive, *beginning on a different pitch*. The sequence usually repeats the intervals and rhythm of the motive. In the example below, the motive is repeated twice, each time moving a step higher in pitch:

From *Sarabanda* (*Scorebook* 65) Corelli

A sequence may also descend in pitch:

From *Minuet* (*Scorebook* 64) Visée

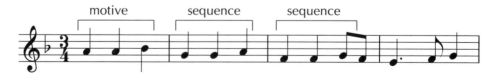

Notice that on the last beat of the second repetition, the rhythm changes from a quarter note to two eighth notes. A sequence invariably gives way to other melodic considerations, in this case the approach to the end of the phrase.

Inversion

Another way that a motive can be developed is by **inversion**, or turning the motive upside down:

Oliver and the Maiden (Scorebook 7)

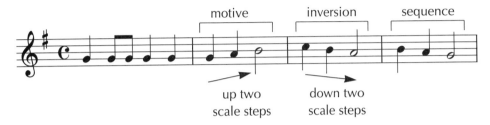

In the example above, the ascending motive in measure 2 is inverted in measure 3, and therefore descends. Measure 4 then repeats the inversion a step lower in pitch, creating a sequence. (Compare this use of the term "inversion" with that on p. 60, where it applies to intervals.)

Motivic Development

The entire process through which a motive repeats and changes is called **motivic development**. As *The Hunter* demonstrates, a motive may contain *different parts* from which a melody unfolds. Or a motive can expand by the addition of new notes. The motive can also be varied by inverting it or using it in sequence. Usually a motive is developed in several ways in a particular melody or musical composition, as in *Oliver and the Maiden*. Sometimes the particular type of variation is not exact but approximate; and sometimes new musical ideas are introduced along with the motivic development. Consider the following melody:

Variation Melody

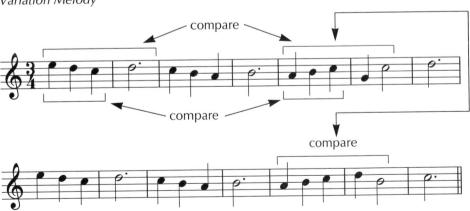

MOTIVE—SUMMARY

Motive: a short musical idea. For example:

Rhythmic Identity: the rhythm of a motive.

Pitch Identity: the order of a motive's pitches.

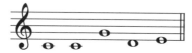

Sequence: the repetition of a motive starting on another pitch.

Inversion: the repetition of a motive with the direction of its intervals reversed.

10   Examine the motivic structure of the following melody. Play each variation in order to hear how the original motive underlies the entire melodic structure. In the space provided under each section of the melody, write a sentence that describes how the motive is varied.

Variation Melody

Variation 1

Write:

Variation 2

Write:

11 Complete the following melodies based on the motive given for each.

a.

b.

TERMS, SYMBOLS, AND CONCEPTS

spelling complex triads
diminished triad
augmented triad
harmonic system
position in key
transposing chords

motive
pitch identity of a motive
rhythmic identity of a motive
motivic development
sequence
inversion

SUGGESTED ACTIVITIES

1. Finish analyzing Schütz's *Psalm 75* (*Scorebook* 77) for triad quality. Some triads are missing one of the chord tones. Write the name of each triad underneath the staff.

2. Analyze Lasso's Prologue from *Prophetiae sibyllarum* (*Scorebook* 76) for triad quality. Write the name of each triad underneath the staff, except for those beats identified with an asterisk (*).

3. Transpose the following songs to the indicated keys. Identify all chords by root and quality and position in key.

   I Know Where I'm Going (*Scorebook* 25) to F

   The Water Is Wide (*Scorebook* 26) to A

4. Choose among the following, and examine them for motive and motivic development.

   Game Song (*Scorebook* 3)

   Brochan Lom (*Scorebook* 6)

   La paloma (*Scorebook* 36)

   The Welcome Song (*Scorebook* 46)

   Morley, *Nancie* (*Scorebook* 61)

Byrd, *Galiarda* (*Scorebook* 62)

Purcell, *Minuet* (*Scorebook* 63)

Corelli, *Sarabanda* (*Scorebook* 65)

Haydn, Theme from *Symphony No. 100* (*Scorebook* 68)

Rossini, *Cujus animam* (*Scorebook* 71)

Beethoven, Theme from *Piano Sonata No. 19* (*Scorebook* 74)

5. Create a motive that is based on a particular rhythmic or pitch identity, or both. Then compose a two-phrase melody based on that motive. Use at least two different ways to develop your motive.

CHAPTER TEN

7th Chords

A **7th chord** is a four-note chord built in 3rds. It is formed by adding a 3rd above the 5th of a triad. The term "7th chord" derives its name from the interval between the root and the highest note, a 7th.

Play:

triad   7th chord   triad   7th chord

Like the triad, the 7th chord falls either on lines or in spaces.

1   Write 7th chords above each note. Do not use accidentals at this time.

Examples

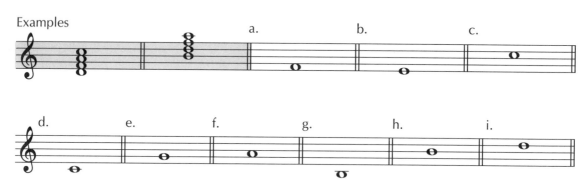

7th-Chord Quality

7th chords can have different qualities, illustrated here by five different 7th chords constructed on D.

minor   dominant   major   diminished   half-diminished
7th   7th   7th   7th   7th

To begin, we will consider three qualities: the dominant 7th chord (V7 chord) the minor 7th chord (m7), and the major 7th chord (M7). We will take up two other types of 7th chords, the diminished 7th (°7) and the half-diminished 7th (ø7), shortly.

The Dominant 7th Chord

The **dominant 7th** (V7) **chord** is widely used in tonal harmony. It takes its name from the 5th scale degree of the major scale, which is called the **dominant**, and occurs naturally when built on this note. For example, the dominant 7th chord in the key of C is spelled:

dominant
7th (V7)

The intervallic structure of the dominant 7th chord consists of a major triad plus a minor 3rd above it. Notice that the interval between the root and 7th of the chord is a minor 7th. Play these dominant 7th chords:

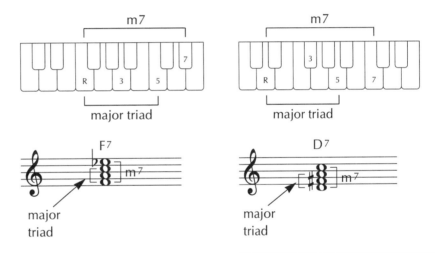

---

2 Write the indicated dominant 7th chords on the staff and keyboard.

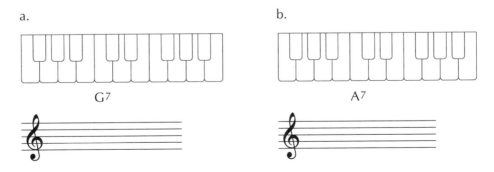

a.

G7

b.

A7

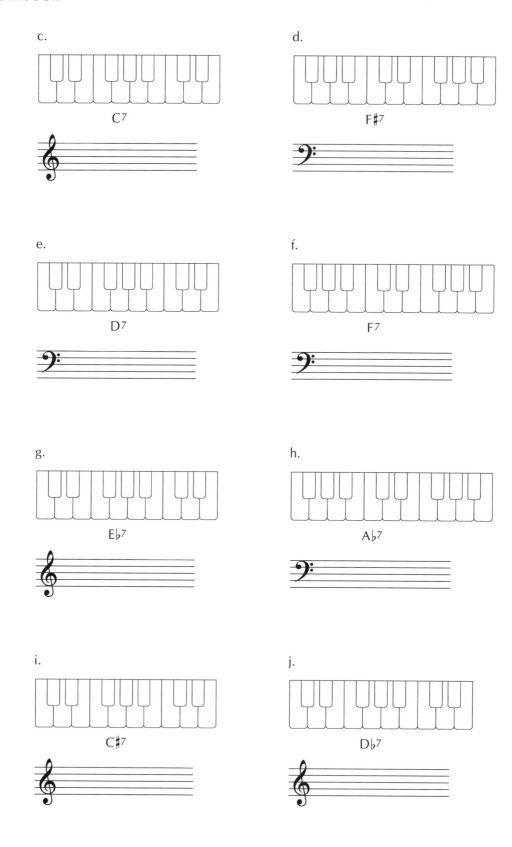

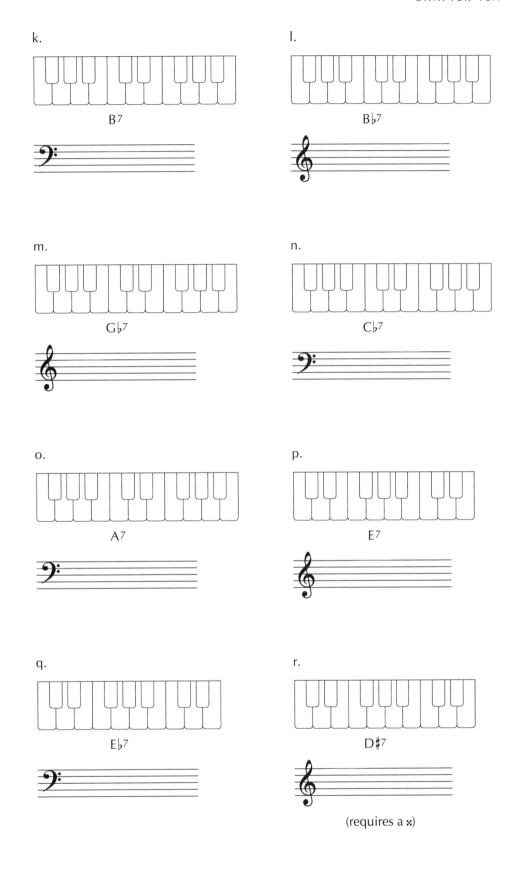

k.

B⁷

l.

B♭⁷

m.

G♭⁷

n.

C♭⁷

o.

A⁷

p.

E⁷

q.

E♭⁷

r.

D♯⁷

(requires a 𝄪)

s.   t.

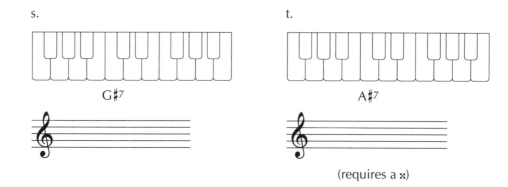

G♯7   A♯7

(requires a 𝄪)

3 Build a dominant 7th chord on the 5th scale degree of each of these major keys. In parentheses, write any sharps or flats that occur in the key signature. Name each chord.

Example:

A⁷

V⁷

a.

b.

c.

d.

e.

f.

g.

h.

i.

j.

Complex Spelling of 7th Chords

When spelling 7th chords, you will find a situation similar to that encountered when spelling complex triads (p. 149). Knowing how to spell one 7th chord can help you spell another one; for example, you can raise or lower the first chord a half step. The following examples concern the dominant 7th chord only, but this process can be applied to all other types of 7th chords.

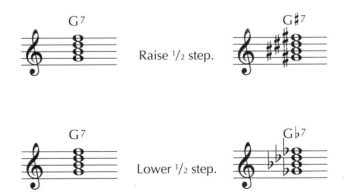

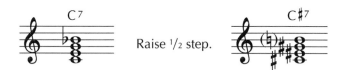

Minor-Scale Triads: Position in Key

When applied to the natural minor scale, the "position in key" concept (see Chapter Nine, p. 154) results in the following triad qualities:

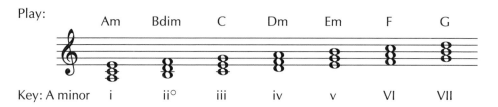

4   In each of the following minor keys, write the required triad. Name the root and quality of each triad in the box provided.

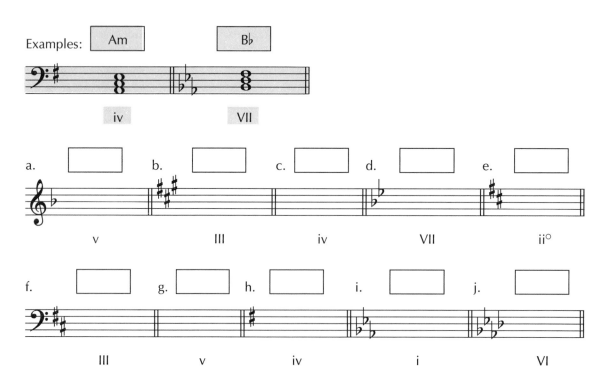

V or V⁷ in a Minor Key

As we observed in Chapter Seven, the melodic patterns of the harmonic minor scale often cause the 7th degree of the scale to be raised to create a leading tone. When this happens in a chordal harmony, the v chord (minor) of the natural minor then becomes a major triad (V). With the addition of a m3 above the 5th of a V chord, a V⁷ chord is formed.

ALTERATION OF THE NATURAL MINOR TO FORM V AND V⁷

5   Write the V and V⁷ chords in the following minor keys. Remember to raise the 3rd of the chord, which is the 7th degree of the minor scale, one half step to produce a leading tone. Write the key signature first.

Example
Key: D minor   a. Key: C minor   b. Key: E minor   c. Key: G minor   d. Key: B minor

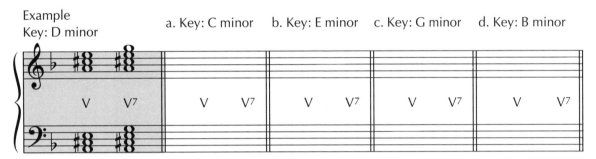

6   Write the V7 chord in the following major or minor keys. Write the key signature first. Notate the chord on the keyboard diagram. Name the chord in the box provided.

Example:
Key: F

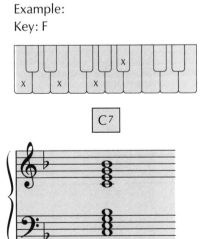

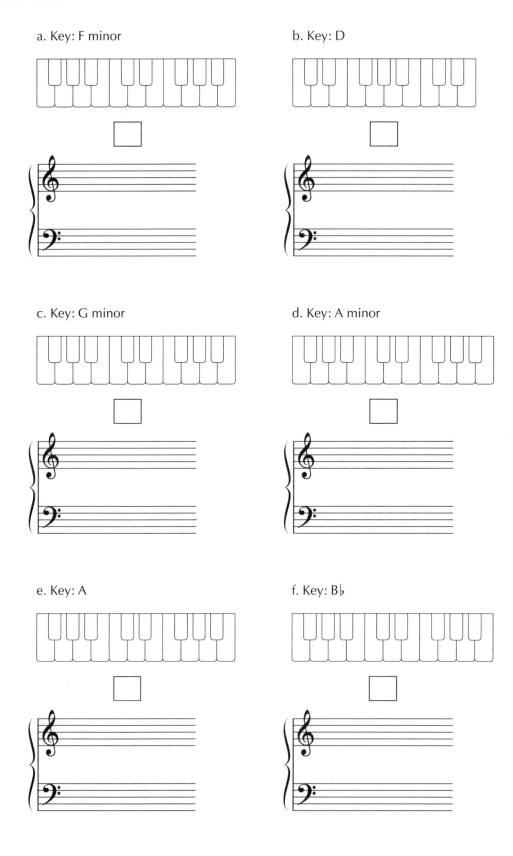

g. Key: B minor

h. Key: E♭

i. Key: A♭

j. Key: B

k. Key: D♭

l. Key: F♯

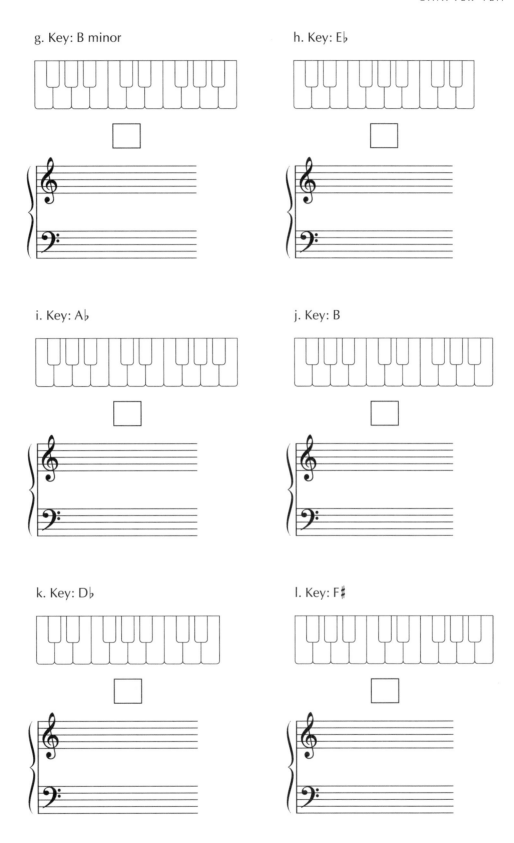

The Minor 7th Chord

Another type of chord results when a 7th chord is built on the 2nd, 3rd, and 6th degrees of the major scale. It is called the **minor 7th chord**.

Notice in the above example that a minor 7th chord may be labeled in two ways: position in key (small Roman numerals plus 7) or root name plus m7. To change a dominant 7th chord into a minor 7th chord, *lower* the third of the chord a half step.

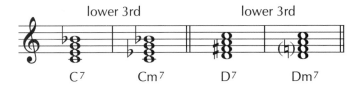

7 Change each of the given chords to the opposite type. If it is a dominant 7th chord, rewrite it as a minor 7th. If it is a minor 7th chord, rewrite it as a dominant 7th. Give the root and quality for all chords.

Example:

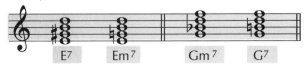

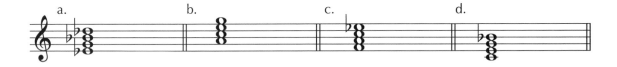

The Major 7th Chord

Building a 7th chord on the 1st and 4th degrees of the major scale produces another chord type: the **major 7th chord**.

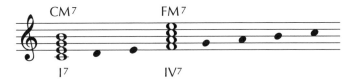

To change a dominant 7th chord into a major 7th chord, simply raise the 7th of the chord a half step to create the interval of a major 7th between the root and 7th of the chord:

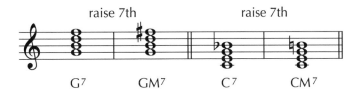

---

8 Name the intervals in the dominant 7th, minor 7th, and major 7th chords given below. Note that C is the root of all the chords. (The first interval is given.)

a.   b.   c.

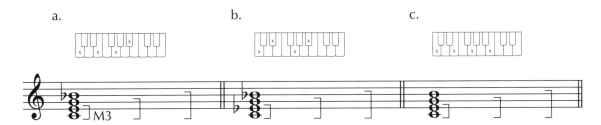

9 Complete the following sentences.

a. To change a dominant 7th chord to a minor 7th chord, _____

_____.

b. To change a dominant 7th chord to a major 7th chord, _____

_____.

c. To change a major 7th chord to a minor 7th chord, _____

_____.

10 On the keyboard and staff, write the 7th chords that are indicated, and write the name of the chord in the box below.

Example:

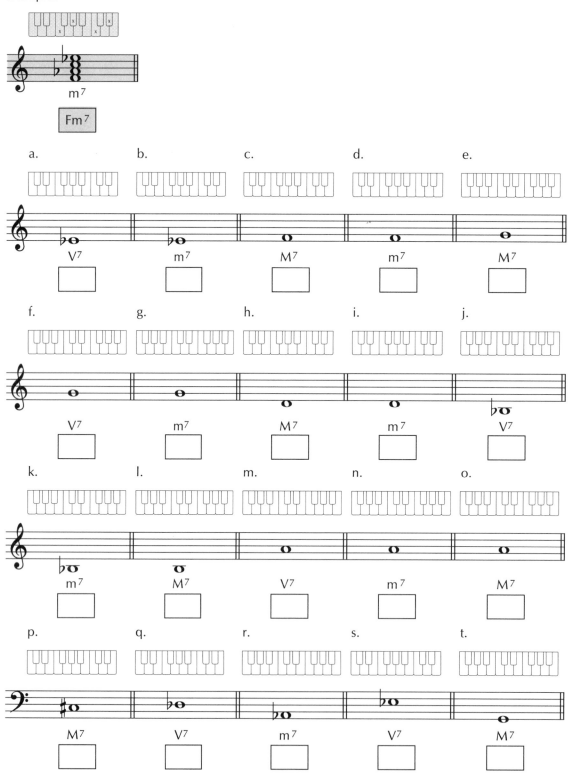

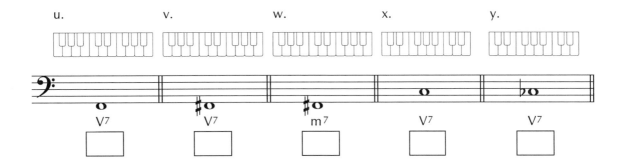

u. v. w. x. y.

V^7 V^7 m^7 V^7 V^7

Diminished and Half-Diminished 7th Chords

Two additional types of chords will complete our study of 7th chords. The **diminished 7th** ($^{\circ}7$) and **half-diminished 7th** ($^{\varnothing}7$) are both formed by adding a 7th to a diminished triad.

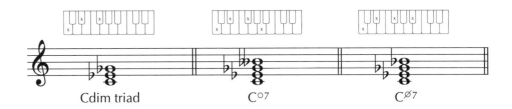

Cdim triad $C^{\circ}7$ $C^{\varnothing}7$

The half-diminished 7th results when the 7th chord is built on the 7th degree of a major scale. Note that the 7th above the root of the chord is a m7.

$B^{\varnothing}7$

$vii^{\varnothing}7$

The diminished 7th (or full diminished 7th, as it is sometimes called) occurs when a 7th chord is built on the raised 7th degree of a minor scale. This chord requires a new interval between the root and 7th of the chord, the diminished 7th. This interval is one half step smaller than a minor 7th.

$B^{\circ}7$

$vii^{\circ}7$

11   Write the indicated 7th chords on both the keyboard and staff. Name each chord. Study the example.

Example:

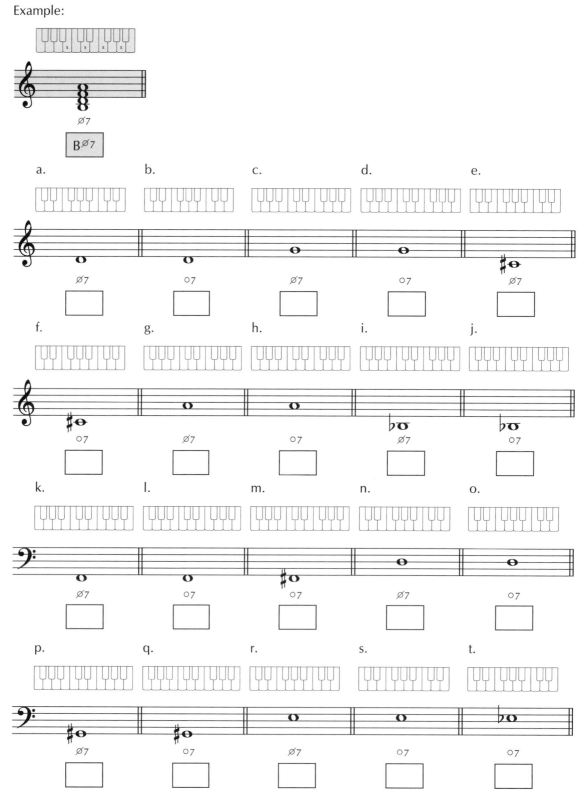

TERMS, SYMBOLS, AND CONCEPTS

7th chord
dominant
dominant 7th chord
construction of a V⁷ chord in a
    major or minor key
minor scale triad quality, position
    in key

minor 7th chord
major 7th chord
diminished 7th chord
half-diminished 7th chord

SUGGESTED ACTIVITIES

1. Examine the following pieces for use of either a v, V, or V⁷ chord.

   The Trees They Do Grow High (*Scorebook* 29)

   Johnny Has Gone for a Soldier (*Scorebook* 34)

   La paloma (*Scorebook* 36)

   The Oak and the Ash (*Scorebook* 35)

2. Transpose the following melodies:

   The Trees They Do Grow High (*Scorebook* 29) to G minor

   En el portal de Belén (*Scorebook* 37) to F minor

   Bach, Chorale Melody from *The Wedding Cantata* (*Scorebook* 58) to E minor

3. Write the names of the 7th chords in the boxes provided (only those with a □⁷ after them) in Mozart's *Minuet* (*Scorebook* 63).

4. Identify any triads or 7th chords outlined in Haydn's Theme from *Symphony No. 103* (*Scorebook* 67).

CHAPTER ELEVEN

Accompaniments to Melodies

In both Western classical and popular music traditions, melodies (or songs) are often provided with background harmonies by one or more instruments or voices. This harmonic background is called a musical **accompaniment**. Listen to several different types of accompaniments for the songs *The Water Is Wide*, *I Know Where I'm Going*, and *En el portal de Belén* (all on Cassette).

The most popular instruments for accompaniment are the keyboard and the guitar. In this chapter, we will concentrate on keyboard accompaniments. You will find material on the guitar as an accompaniment instrument in Appendix VII.

Keyboard Accompaniments

The keyboard provides many possibilities for harmonic accompaniments. The following excerpt illustrates one of the most common accompaniment patterns: the arpeggio.

The melody in the excerpt above is played by a violin. Both the cello and the piano provide the accompaniment. The right hand of the piano part (treble clef) features a series of chords that are broken up into individual tones. This broken-chord pattern is called an **arpeggio**, and is one of the compositional devices we will learn to use in this chapter.

1 Write out the melody with accompaniment of the Haydn *Trio*, putting each arpeggiated chord in its basic root position. The anacrusis and first measure are completed for you. Name the root and quality of each left-hand chord.

Voice Leading

In conventional keyboard accompaniments, chords are written according to the concept of good **voice leading**. Every chord tone is considered a separate part or voice whose movement from one chord to another follows a coherent melodic pattern. Smooth voice leading results when the notes of a chord move mostly in step-wise motion, as in the upper two voices of the following example:

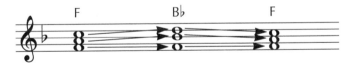

2 The following accompaniment patterns are derived from the model above. The arrows point out the smooth, stepwise movement of each voice. Study and play:

a.

b.

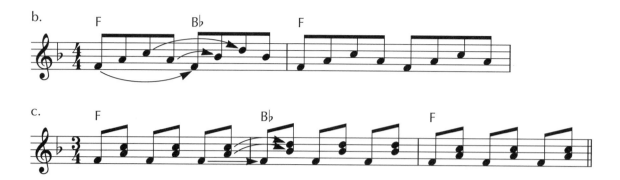

c.

Common Tone

In each of the three accompaniment patterns given in exercise #2, the voices move to the same pitches even though the rhythm changes. The top C always goes to D and then returns to C; the middle A moves to B♭ and returns to A; the lowest F stays on F, since that pitch is common to both chords. A pitch that is shared by two different chords is called a **common tone**. In the chord voicing above, the pitch F is a common tone.

3   Identify the common tones in these exercises by drawing horizontal lines between them. Name all chords.

Example:

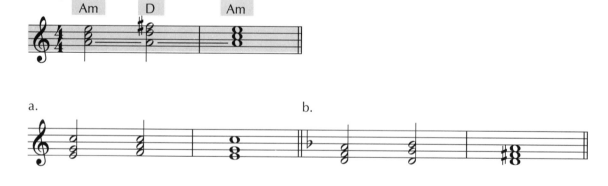

e.   f.

Voicing the V⁷

A popular chord progression for keyboard accompaniments uses the I, IV, and V⁷ chords. In the voicing that is illustrated below, notice that the V⁷ is incomplete (no 5th). Play:

4   Transpose the voicing in the illustration above to D, F, and E♭, writing the key signatures first. Name the chords.

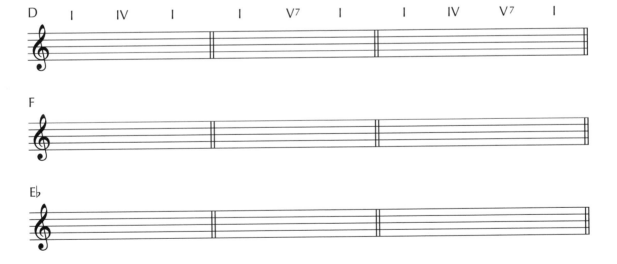

Voicing V⁷ in a Minor Key

The voicing of this chord progression in a minor key is the same as the voicing in a major key. The 3rd of the V chord is raised so that the quality of the chord is a dominant 7th.

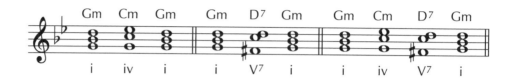

Adding the Bass

By adding the root of the chord in the left hand, you can complete the harmonic progression.

Key: G minor   Key: G major

Here are some patterns derived from the two examples above. Observe that in the V⁷ chord, the 5th is omitted and the root is doubled.

5 Continue these accompaniment patterns using the voicings of the chords shown above.

a.

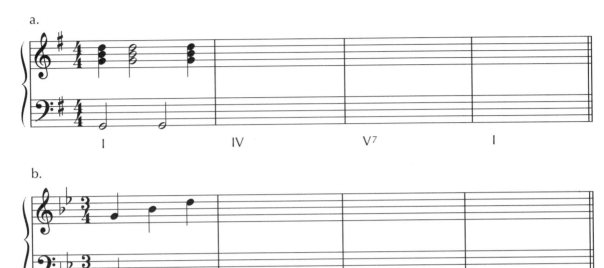

Additional Voicings of I, IV, and V⁷

Here are two other voicings of the I, IV, and V⁷ chords. Compare them with the examples given previously. Observe which voices share a common tone.

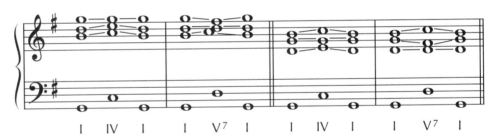

6 Following are some traditional types of accompaniment patterns using the I, IV, and V⁷ chords. Again, the 5th of the V⁷ is not used, in order to create smoother voice leading. Name the keys and chords. Play:

a.

b.

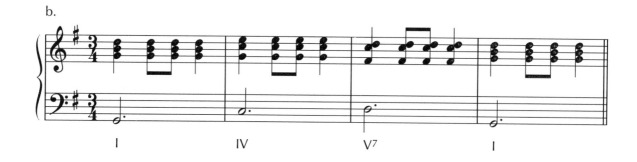

c.

7 Finish this piano accompaniment using the same rhythmic pattern in each measure.

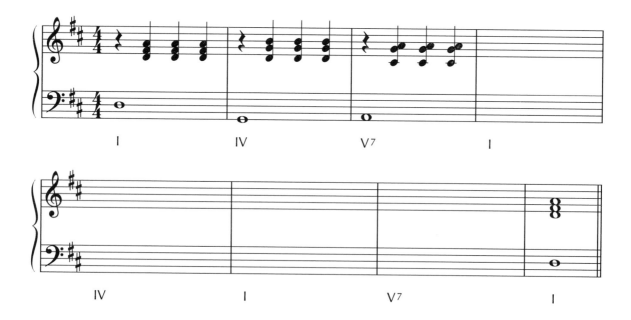

8 Finish this piano accompaniment using the same rhythmic pattern in each measure. You may end the accompaniment pattern in the last measure however you wish. Compare with exercise #7: this exercise is in the _____ minor key of #7.

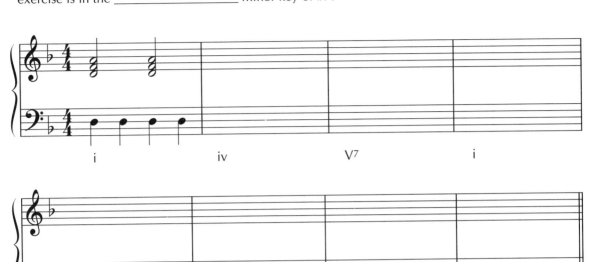

9 Using the same progression as in exercise #8, write an accompaniment that continues the motive shown in the first measure.

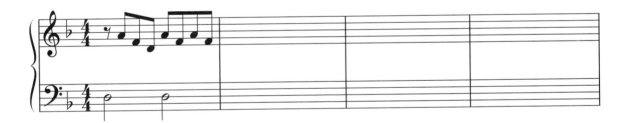

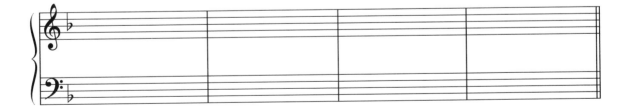

10   Finish this accompaniment pattern for *Silent Night* (*Scorebook*, 38). Circle all the nonchord tones in the melody.

Using V
Instead of V7

Often, V and V7 are interchangeable, the choice of one or the other being a matter of taste. Compare the two chord progressions below:

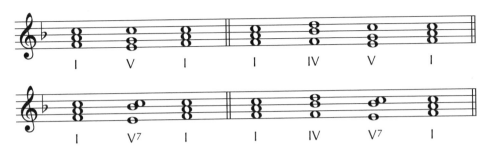

Notice that when a IV chord moves to a V, *there are no common tones*. Although not all chord progressions contain common tones, most can show good stepwise voice leading, as the examples above illustrate.

11 Complete these accompaniment patterns.

a.

b.

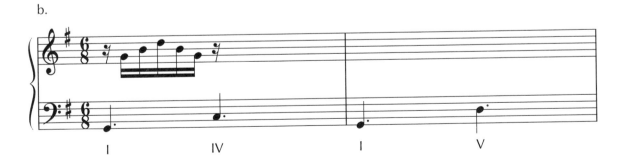

Harmonizing with the vi Chord

The next exercise includes a vi chord, which is also commonly used in tonal. music. For this exercise, use one of the following voicings as a model for your accompaniment.

Key: G major

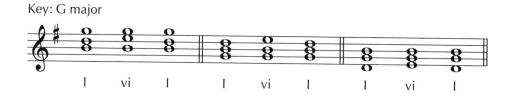

I   vi   I   I   vi   I   I   vi   I

---

12 Write the root and quality of the given chords under each Roman numeral. Choose an accompaniment pattern, either your own or one from a previous example. Write an accompaniment.

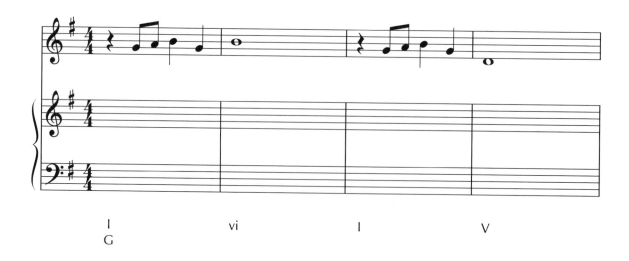

I   vi   I   V
G

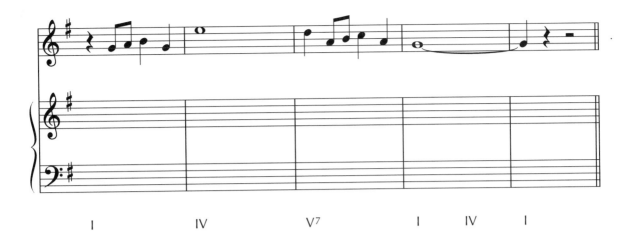

I   IV   V⁷   I   IV   I

Harmonizing with the ii Chord

The next exercise uses a ii chord, which is often followed by a IV chord. Follow one of these voicings in your accompaniment.

I   ii   IV   I   ii   IV   I   ii   IV

You will notice that there are no common tones between the I and ii chords. The ii chord, however, shares two common tones with the IV chord.

13   In the following exercise, write the root and quality of the given chords under each Roman numeral. Choose a pattern for the accompaniment, either your own or one presented above. Write the accompaniment. Then compose a melody—either a chord melody or one that contains some nonchord tones—and write it on the upper staff.

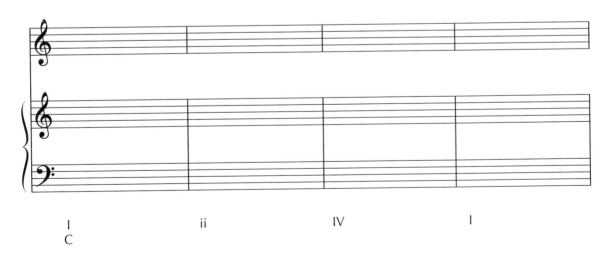

I   ii   IV   I
C

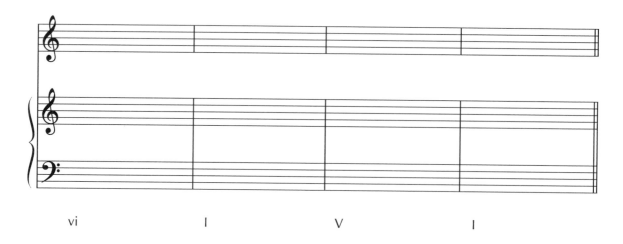

vi   I   V   I

Tonality and the V or V⁷

Harmonic progressions play an important role in establishing key centers. In our discussions of major and minor scales, we observed how recognizable scale patterns can cause a pitch to be heard as the tonic. In the same way, recognizable harmonic progressions can cause the listener to focus on one chord as the tonic chord. Different progressions have varying effects on tonality. Traditionally, the strongest harmonic progression for establishing the tonic chord as key center is V–I or V⁷–I, caused by the pull of the leading tone in the V or V⁷ chord toward the tonic.

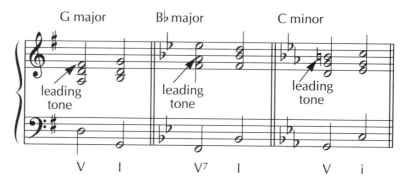

Modulation

The progression of V–I or V⁷–I creates such a strong tonal effect that it is often used to establish a different key center within a piece by the introduction of a new V–I relationship. This change of key center is called **modulation**. Observe the modulation from the key of A major to E major in the following melody.

Key: E major

This melody modulates through the B and B⁷ chords, which are V and V⁷ in the key of E major. Notice in the last line that the modulation requires accidentals that would occur only in the new key.

How to Harmonize a Melody

When choosing a harmonic background for a melody, keep in mind the following points:

1. To begin, figure out the key of the melody and the chords in that key.
2. You can harmonize many simple songs by using the I, IV, and V (or V⁷) chords in major, and the i, iv, and V (or V⁷) chords in minor. Some require only I and V.
3. Important pitches such as the tonic and dominant, pitches that last a long time, those that fall on the beat, or pitches that begin or end phrases may be I, IV, or V chord tones. As a starting point, try different combinations of these chords that fit the important tones of the melody.
4. If you have found places where the I, IV, and V chords fit, sing through the melody while playing these chords, leaving empty harmonic places where they do not fit. Experiment by adding other chords (for example, the ii, iii, or vi chords) in these empty moments.
5. If you think the melody modulates to a new key, try the V or V⁷ chords of the new key at the point of modulation.

There are many ways to harmonize a given melody. You may even discover that chords totally outside the key may work. In the final analysis, your ear will be the judge. The points given above are only to start you off on your discovery of harmony.

Parallelism in Modern Accompaniments

In our study of voicing and chord progressions, we observed traditional concepts of good voice leading. Another type of voice leading, called **parallelism**, is found frequently in both classical and popular music of the twentieth century. Parallelism results when the harmony changes but the voicing remains exactly the same.

PARALLEL VOICINGS

Voice Leading in Popular Styles

In classical music composed before the twentieth century, parallelism was not considered good voice leading. Contemporary popular music, however, combines parallelism and the traditional voice-leading practices described earlier in this chapter. The examples below demonstrate some possible voicings for contemporary styles. (See also Appendix VI: "How to Read a Lead Sheet.") All parallel voicings are indicated by lines.

14 Write the following accompaniment patterns. You may use parallel voicings where appropriate. In places that are marked with an asterisk (*), make sure your voicing uses common tones. Review 7th chords in Chapter Ten before you do the exercises.

a.

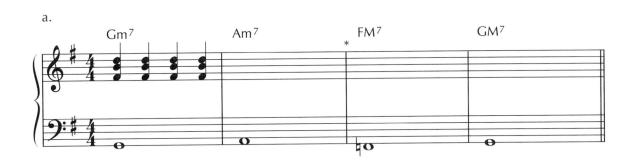

b.

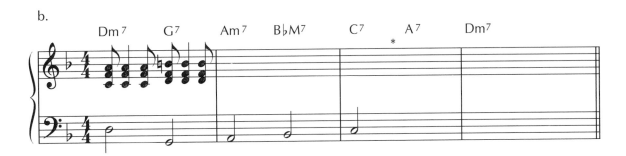

c. Choose your own pattern:

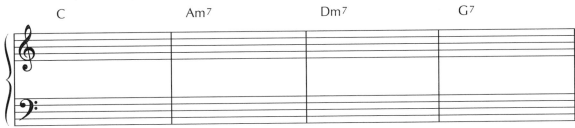

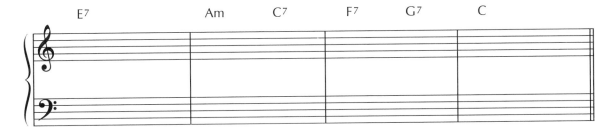

d.

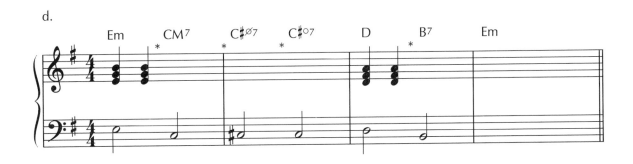

e. Choose your own pattern:

TERMS, SYMBOLS, AND CONCEPTS

accompaniment	use of vi chords
arpeggio	use of ii chords
voice leading	modulation
common tone	parallelism
use of V or V^7	modern accompaniments

SUGGESTED ACTIVITIES

1. Write accompaniments for some of the following melodies that use I and V^7 (major) or i and V^7 (minor). Use traditional voice leading.

   Game Song (*Scorebook* 3)

   Fray Diego (*Scorebook* 4)

   O du schöner Rosengarten (*Scorebook* 5)

2. Write an accompaniment for *Carraig Aonair* (*Scorebook* 19) using i and v (minor).

3. Write accompaniments for the following melodies that use I, IV, and V7.

   Philis, plus avare que tendre (*Scorebook* 8)

   Die Gedanken sind frei (*Scorebook* 9)

   Brahms, *Lullaby* (*Scorebook* 55)

4. Write accompaniments to some of the following songs that use a variety of chords.

   Drink to Me Only with Thine Eyes (*Scorebook* 28)

   Brocham Lom (*Scorebook* 6)

   Que ne suis-je la fougère (*Scorebook* 15)

   In dem Weiten stand ein Haus (*Scorebook* 20)

5. Identify and modulation in:

   Jeune fillette (*Scorebook* 16)

   The Oak and the Ash (*Scorebook* 35)

6. Use one of the chord progressions in Appendix V to compose a melody and accompaniment that combines parallelism with traditional voice leading.

CHAPTER TWELVE

Modes

In its broadest sense, the term **mode** designates a type of scale that is diatonic in arrangement. Like the major and natural minor scales, modes have five whole steps and two half steps. What distinguishes one mode from another is the position of the two half steps. Modes can be used as the basis for both melody and harmony. Such music is characterized as **modal**.

1 Play the following modes.

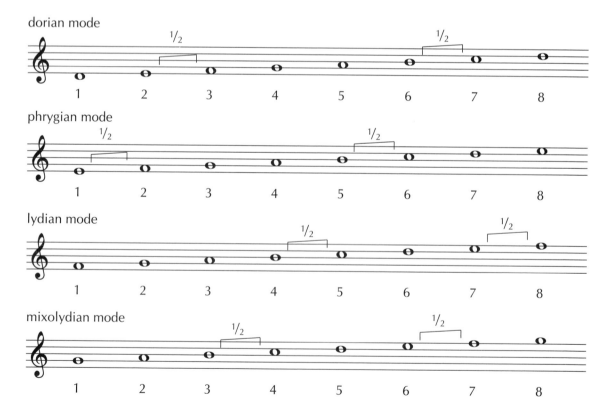

dorian mode

phrygian mode

lydian mode

mixolydian mode

2 Play these modal examples.

a. dorian   Hymn tune

b. phrygian   Hymn tune

c. lydian   English folk tune

d. mixolydian   Gregorian chant

Ve - ni Cre - a - tor___ Spi - ri - tus, Men - tes

tu - o - rum vi - si - ta: Im - ple___ su - per - na___

gra - ti - a, Quae___ tu cre - a - sti_____ pec - to - ra.

SCALES AND MODES: PATTERNS OF STEPS

Major, natural minor, and traditional modes contain five whole steps and two half steps. The position of the half steps is as follows:

Major: half steps between 3 and 4, 7 and 8.
Minor: half steps between 2 and 3, 5 and 6.
Dorian: half step between 2 and 3, 6 and 7.
Phrygian: half steps between 1 and 2, 5 and 6.
Lydian: half steps between 4 and 5, 7 and 8.
Mixolydian: half steps between 3 and 4, 6 and 7.

3   Although the model for the modes is usually given on the white keys of the piano, a mode can have any note as its tonic. Using the half-step/whole-step pattern given above, write the following modes as indicated. Use accidentals, not key signatures. Bracket the half steps (remember that any step that is not bracketed is a whole step). Alternate between treble and bass clefs.

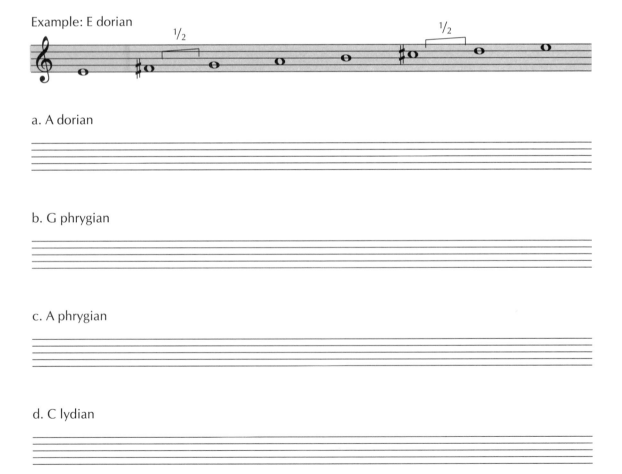

Example: E dorian

a. A dorian

b. G phrygian

c. A phrygian

d. C lydian

e. D lydian

f. D mixolydian

g. G mixolydian

h. C mixolydian

4 Embellish the following chord melodies with the requested nonchord tones. You may wish to review composing a chord melody (p. 140), passing tones (p. 143), and neighbor tones (p. 142). Study the possible embellishments in the examples carefully.

    a. Add passing tones between some of the chord tones of this melody in the dorian mode. Study the examples of the first measure. Write the new version of the melody on the staves provided below. Do not forget the clef and time signature:

Example:

Original

Possible embellishments

Melody: dorian mode

b. Add upper or lower neighbor notes and passing tones to embellish this melody in the mixolydian mode, made up of whole notes. Study the examples of the first measure. Write the new version of the melody on the staves provided below. Do not forget the clef and time signature:

Example:

Original

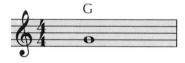

Possible embellishments

Melody: mixolydian mode

Scale and Mode Mixture

Many melodies and larger musical compositions are based on a mixture of various scales and modes. Examining music that features such a mixture can give us a deeper understanding of tonality. Each of the following melodies combines various scales and modes:

1. *Greensleeves* (*Scorebook* 33)

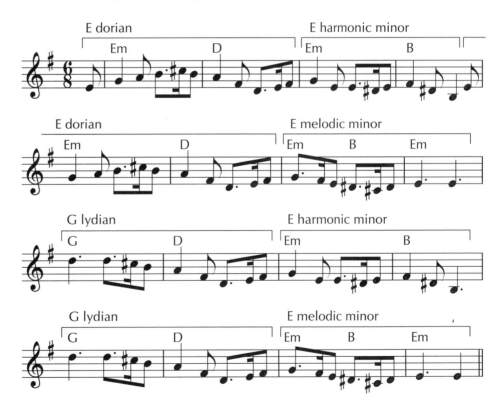

2. *Remember, O Thou Man (Scorebook 77)*   Ravenscroft

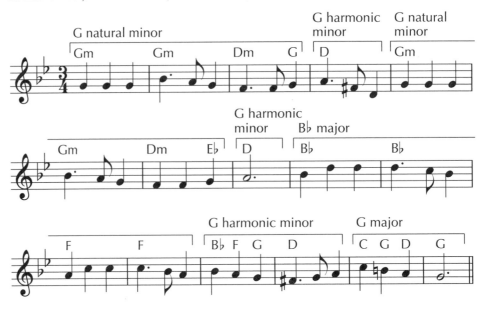

Although both of the melodies above use a mixture of scales and modes, the tonality of each is never in doubt. The dorian mode and the harmonic and melodic minor scales in *Greensleeves* all have E as their tonic. The two middle phrases of *Greensleeves*, which begin in the lydian mode on G (remember that G is the relative major of E minor), both quickly return to E minor: E harmonic minor the first time and E melodic minor at the end of the song.

Remember, O Thou Man predominantly uses the G–natural minor and G–harmonic minor scales. Although the middle phrase of the melody is in B♭ major (the relative major of G minor), the final measures return to G major (the parallel major of G minor). Thus, G is heard clearly as the tonal center of the piece. These examples demonstrate how composers can use various combinations of scales and modes *while retaining one key center.*

Pentatonic Scale

The world of music includes melodies based on many types of scales, not just the traditional ones that we have focused on in this book. Not all scales throughout the world contain seven notes. There are some melodies based on scales made up of only three notes. A five-note scale is the basis for *Cherry Blooms*, a Japanese melody (*Scorebook* 12). Five-note, or **pentatonic**, scales are used in many areas of the world. Here are two kinds of pentatonic scales:

PENTATONIC SCALES

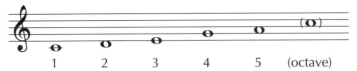

1   2   3   4   5   (octave)

1   2   3   4   5   (octave)

5 Write out the scales that are used in each of the following pieces from the *Scorebook*. Where possible, use the tone that sounds like the tonic as the beginning note (sometimes this is not always clear).

Example: *Cherry Blooms* (*Scorebook* 12)

a. *Song of the Crow* (*Scorebook* 10)

b. *Group Song* (*Scorebook* 2)

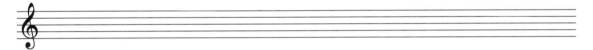

c. *Hymn* (Armenian) (*Scorebook* 22)

**Form:
Phrase Design**

In Chapter Five, we studied melodies comprised of two or more phrases, each ending with a cadence. We will learn two types of cadences in this section, one that stops the melodic motion temporarily, in the manner of a comma at the end of a phrase in a spoken sentence, and one that stops the melodic motion in a more definitive way, much like a period at the end of a sentence. Then, we will examine the way the musical ideas of each phrase help to create the form of a melody.

6   Read aloud the text of *Dear Willie* (*Scorebook* 30).

> A walking and a talking, a walking go I,
> For to meet my dear Willie, I'll meet him by and by.
>
> For to meet him is a pleasure, but parting is grief.
> And a false hearted lover is worse than a thief.
>
> For a thief he will rob you and take what you have
> But a false hearted lover will lead you to the grave.
>
> And the grave will consume you and turn you to dust.
> Not one boy in twenty a poor girl can trust.
>
> A walking and a talking, a walking go I,
> For to meet my dear Willie, I'll meet him by and by.

Each verse of *Dear Willie* has a two-phrase design. How do these phrases relate to each other? Speak the first phrase and stop. Notice the sense of incompletion. Now continue with the second phrase. Once spoken, you sense poetic balance and completion. The same relationship—that of balance and completion—can be heard in the music. Listen to *Dear Willie* (Cassette) and follow its two-phrase design.

The Period

Two musical phrases dependent on each other for balance are called a **period**. The first phrase is the **antecedent**, and the second phrase is the **consequent**. What unites these two phrases is the need for the antecedent phrase to be balanced and completed by the consequent phrase. One determinant of this relationship is the type of cadence at the end of each phrase.

Two Types of Cadences

A **half cadence** is a point of rest at the end of a musical phrase, but one that seems temporary or incomplete. The half cadence creates a desire for more musical motion to balance the first, or antecedent, phrase. A half cadence ends on a note other than the tonic.

A **full cadence** is a point of rest at the end of a consequent phrase that seems complete and final. A full cadence almost always ends on the tonic.

Melodic Aspects of Cadential Design

In the **cadential design** of *Dear Willie*, we find that phrase I ends with a half cadence on the note C, the dominant in the key of F minor. Phrase II ends with a full cadence on F, the tonic and key center of F minor.

***DEAR WILLIE*—PERIOD**

The two phrases depend upon each other for balance: antecedent phrase, consequent phrase. For this reason, the form of each verse of *Dear Willie* is a period.

Double Period

The Trees They Do Grow High (*Scorebook* 29), in contrast, consists of four phrases rather than two. Each four-measure phrase results in a cadence through the steady rhythmic flow. The two-plus-two phrase structure of this melody results in a form called a **double period**. Note that the first period of this double period ends with a half cadence rather than a full cadence.

***THE TREES THEY DO GROW HIGH*—DOUBLE PERIOD**

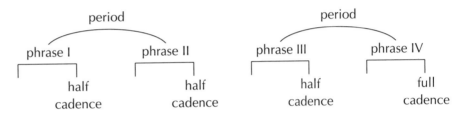

The symmetrical design above is a distinguishing aspect of the double period. Many four-phrase melodies are not double periods.

7   Play *The Trees They Do Grow High*. Following the diagram that is given above, answer the following questions.

a. On which degrees of the A-minor scale do the half cadences of the song occur? _____

_____

b. On what scale degree does the full cadence occur? _____

The Design of Phrase Forms

Cadences are not the only determinant of a piece's form. Another is the melodic material used. One of the first things we listen for is the repetition of a phrase or melodic motive. Sometimes phrases begin with a new motive to create contrast. The melodic shapes of the phrases also can differ. When all of these aspects of a melody are heard in combination, we perceive the melody's overall form.

Labeling Phrases   We can label the different phrases of a melody in terms of similar or contrasting melodic patterns, motivic material, melodic shape, and types of cadence. The first phrase is always labeled **a**. The following phrases, if the same as the **a** phrase, are also labeled **a**. If the melodic material contrasts, a new letter name is given: **b** for the first phrase that contrasts with **a**, **c** for the next that contrasts with *both* **a** and **b**, and so forth. If some of the later phrases that occur in the melody are the same as those that were heard earlier, then they share the same letter name.

8   Listen to or play the following melodies.

a. Play *Au clair de la lune*:

Notice that this melody is made up of four phrases. Phrases I, II, and IV are all the same; phrase III is different. This design is indicated in the following way:

phrase I: **a**
phrase II: **a**
phrase III: **b**
phrase IV: **a**

Add the appropriate letter at the beginning of each phrase in the music above.

b. Listen to *Greensleeves* (*Scorebook* 33; Cassette). Notice that the second phrase is a modified repeat of the first. It is therefore labeled **a′** (pronounced "a prime"). The third phrase introduces new melodic material. The fourth phrase is a modified repeat of the third. This phrase design can be diagrammed in the following way:

***Greensleeves*—Phrase design**

phrase I: **a**
phrase II: **a′** (almost the same as I)
phrase III: **b** (new music)
phrase IV: **b′** (almost the same as III)

Phrase design: **a a′ b b′**

c. Now play *The Trees They Do Grow High* (*Scorebook* 29), and observe the phrase design:

***The Trees They Do Grow High*—Phrase design**

phrase I: **a**
phrase II: **a′**
phrase III: **a**
phrase IV: **b**

Phrase design: **a a′ a b**

Parallel and Contrasting Periods

When two phrases start the same way, they are called **parallel**; when they start differently, they are **contrasting**. We designate a parallel period as **a a** or **a a′**—*Melody* (Finnish) (*Scorebook* 14) is an example of the latter. A contrasting period is labeled **a b**. *Dear Willie* (*Scorebook* 30) is a good example.

9 The following pieces are all periods. Examine each to decide whether they are parallel or contrasting.

O du schöner Rosengarten (*Scorebook* 5)
Sleep Gently (*Scorebook* 32)
All the Stars (*Scorebook* 52)
Carraig Aonair (*Scorebook* 19)
Haydn, Theme from *Symphony No. 100* (*Scorebook* 68)
Weber, *Hunter's Theme* from *Der Freischütz* (*Scorebook* 70)

The Three-Phrase Period

A piece made up of three phrases of which the third phrase serves as antecedent to the first two is called a **three-phrase period**. An example of this phrase structure is the Christmas carol *Silent Night*, in which the beginning of all three phrases contrast with each other.

---

10   Play *Silent Night* (*Scorebook* 38), and follow this diagram of the phrase design:

phrase I	phrase II	phrase III
a	**b**	**c**

Flexibility of Form Designations

The melodic forms we have observed are all rather simple, and apply only to certain melodies. Although they could not begin to identify all of the melodies found in music, they can serve as a starting point for considering melodic design. Some melodies are much more complicated structurally; others may appear as unclassifiable using the methods described above.

A Summary of Melodic Design

We have examined several aspects of melodic design thus far:

1. steps, skips, and leaps (p. 59);
2. phrase and cadence (p. 77);
3. melodic shape (p. 78);
4. harmonic background (p. 139);
5. nonchord tones (p. 142);
6. motive and motivic development (p. 160); and
7. period forms (p. 210).

Studying these topics reveals a large part of the underlying structure of melody, but it is important to understand that composers rarely write melodies from a consciously theoretical basis. As you continue to study the actual melodies given in the *Scorebook*, be aware that these melodies present a variety of compositional techniques sometimes beyond the theoretical analyses offered in this book. While dissecting a melody can tell us much about the underlying design, it must not distract us from experiencing the melody as a whole.

Composing Melodies

The above is especially true when composing. We may start from a theoretical stance, but ultimately we seek a compositional skill in which the separate parts of the theoretical design do not inhibit the natural unfolding of a melody. The creative impulse often leads in unpredictable directions. As you work through the following composition exercises, remember that the instructions are only a way to get started. Your ear is the final judge of what you write.

11   Compose melodies according to the following instructions. You may wish to sketch your ideas on the staves provided in the back of this book before you compose the melody in the space provided below.

a. Compose a parallel period in the key of E major:

b. Compose a contrasting period in the key of D minor:

c. Compose a double period in which a motive is developed in various ways. Use either a major or minor key:

TERMS, SYMBOLS, AND CONCEPTS

dorian mode
phrygian mode
lydian mode
mixolydian mode
pentatonic scale
period
antecedent phrase

consequent phrase
half cadence
full cadence
double period
contrasting period
three-phrase period

SUGGESTED ACTIVITIES

1. Examine the following for type of period form:

   Game Song (*Scorebook* 3)

   Fray Diego (*Scorebook* 4)

   Cradle Song (*Scorebook* 13)

   Que ne suis-je la fougère (*Scorebook* 15)

2. Examine for mode or scale and form:

   O'er the Burn, Bessie (*Scorebook* 17)

   Hymn (Armenian) (*Scorebook* 22)

3. Examine for form:

   Beethoven, *Ode to Joy* (*Scorebook* 59)

   Byrd, *Galiarda* (*Scorebook* 62)

   Haydn, Theme from *Symphony No. 100* (*Scorebook* 68)

   Haydn, Theme from *Symphony No. 103* (*Scorebook* 67)

   Weber, *Hunter's Theme* from *Der Freischütz* (*Scorebook* 70)

   Beethoven, Theme from *Piano Sonata No. 19* (*Scorebook* 74)

4. Make up a harmonic background for a two-phrase period (or choose one from Appendix V). Then compose a melody and keyboard accompaniment.

5. Choose a short poem or poetic excerpt. After considering the structure of the poem, write a melody for the words.

REVIEW EXERCISES

Use the exercises that follow as both a review and summary of your work in this book. Refer to past chapters as needed.

1 Write the indicated scales without key signatures.

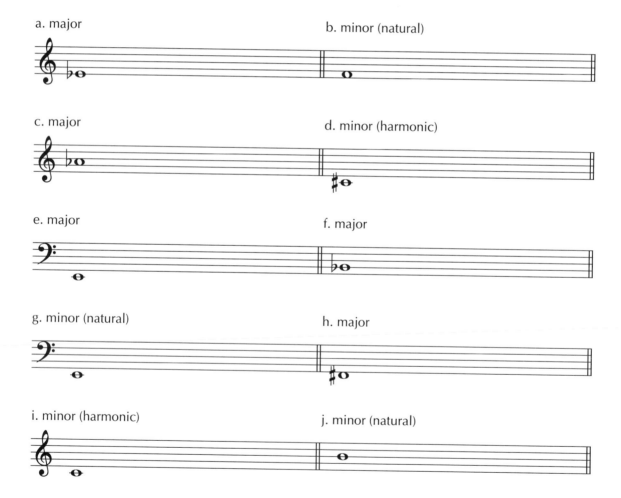

a. major

b. minor (natural)

c. major

d. minor (harmonic)

e. major

f. major

g. minor (natural)

h. major

i. minor (harmonic)

j. minor (natural)

2 Write the following key signatures.

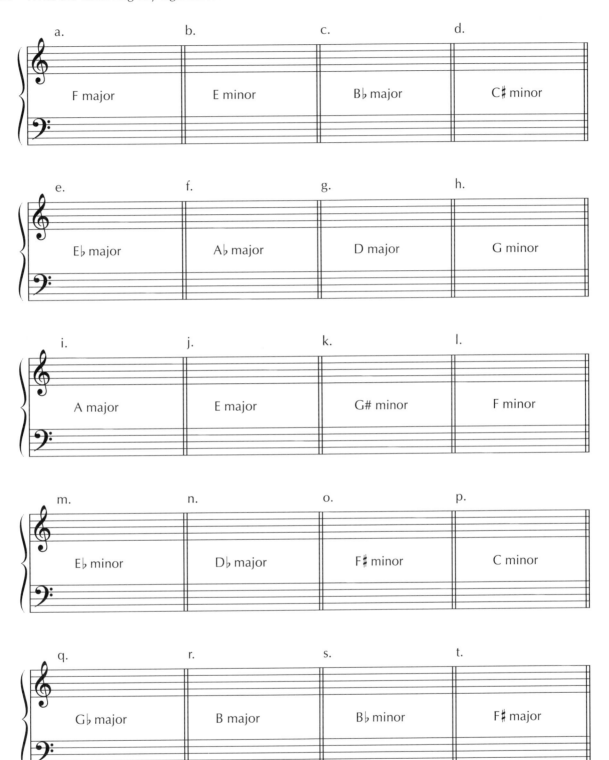

a. F major   b. E minor   c. B♭ major   d. C♯ minor

e. E♭ major   f. A♭ major   g. D major   h. G minor

i. A major   j. E major   k. G# minor   l. F minor

m. E♭ minor   n. D♭ major   o. F♯ minor   p. C minor

q. G♭ major   r. B major   s. B♭ minor   t. F♯ major

3 Using key signatures, write the following minor scales in both clefs.

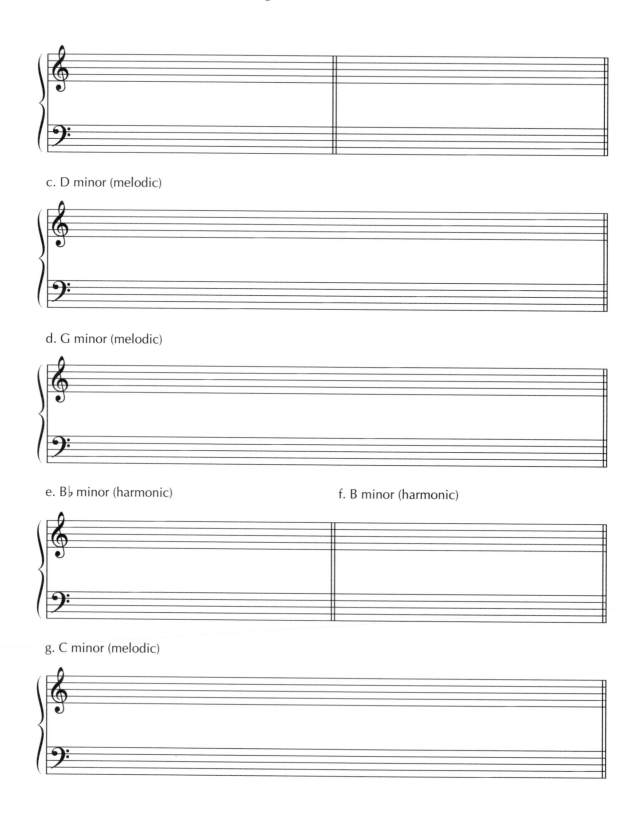

c. D minor (melodic)

d. G minor (melodic)

e. B♭ minor (harmonic)   f. B minor (harmonic)

g. C minor (melodic)

h. F♯ minor (melodic)

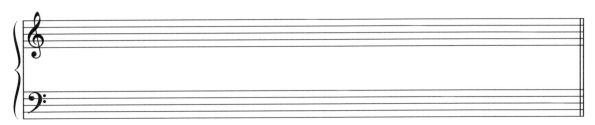

4 Name these intervals.

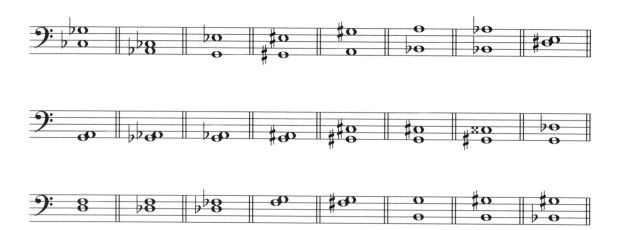

5 Write the note that completes the indicated interval above the given note.

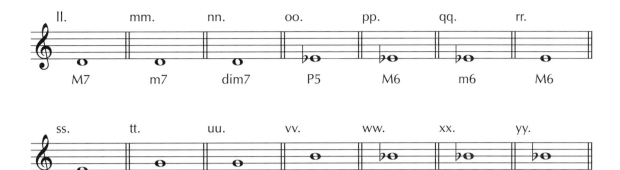

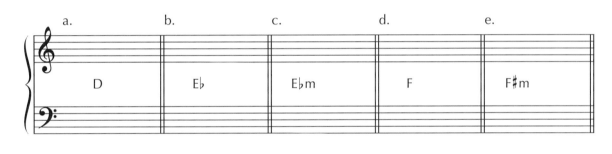

6 Write the correct triad in both clefs.

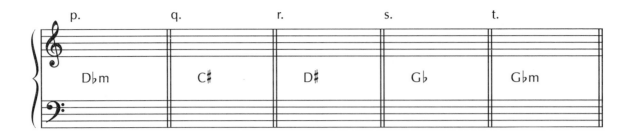

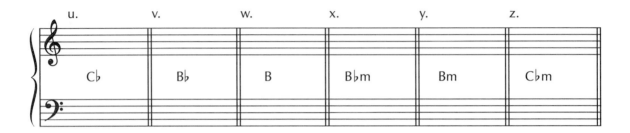

7   Write a major, minor, diminished, and augmented triad on each note.

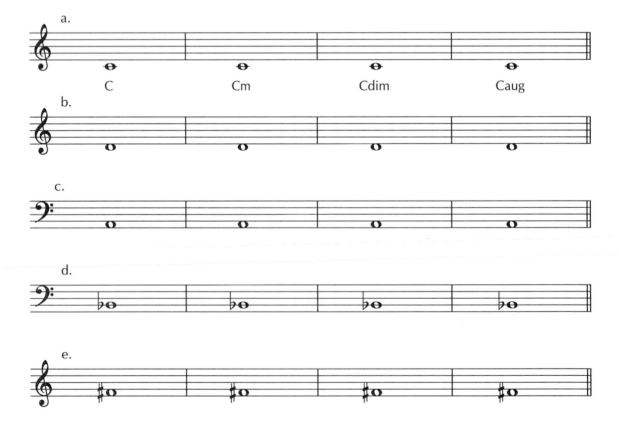

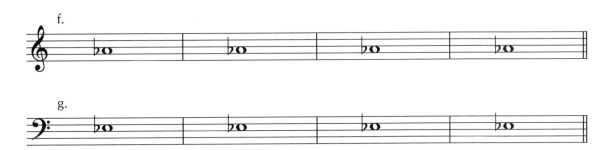

8 Write the indicated 7th chord.

9 Write the indicated chords in the major key of the signature. Name the root and quality.

10 Write the indicated chords in the minor key of the signature. Name the root and quality.

11 Transpose to the indicated key. Use key signatures.

a.

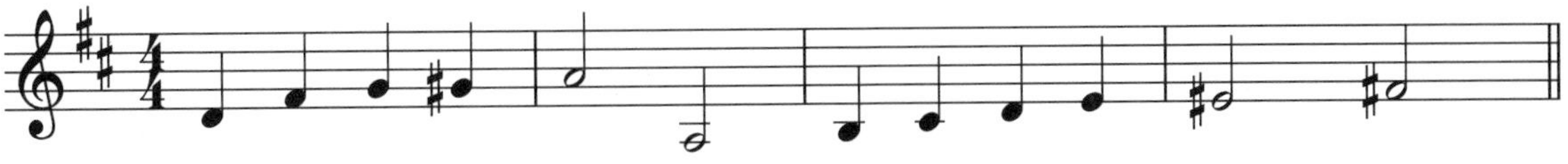

down to B♭

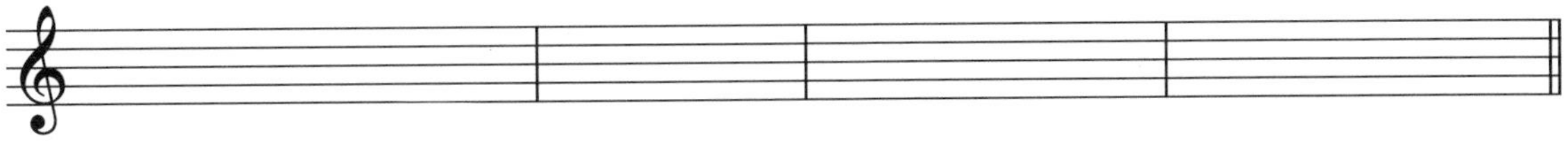

up to A

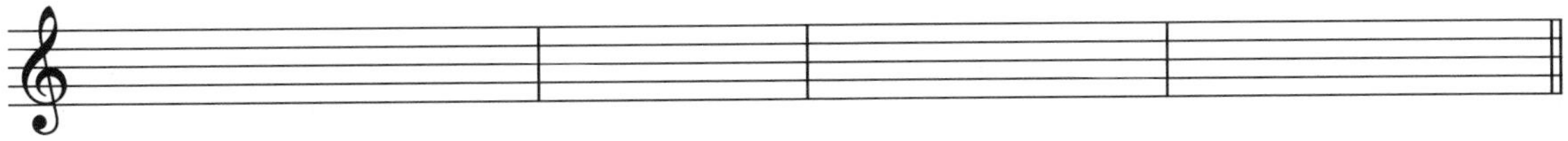

b.

up to B

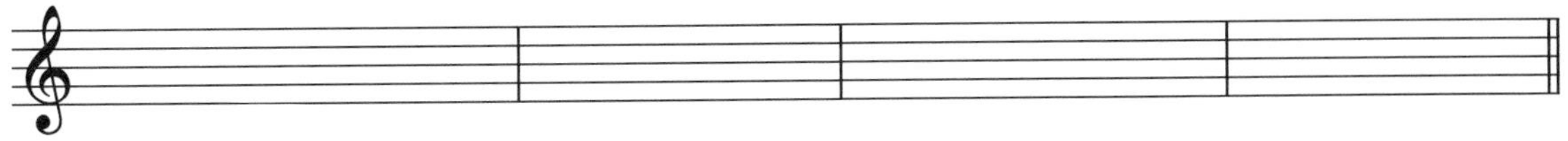

up to F

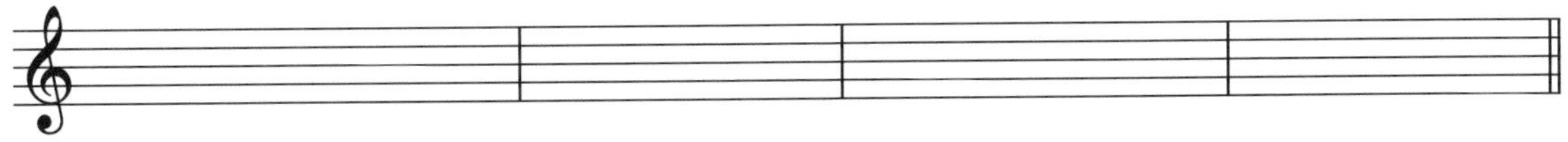

c.

down to B minor

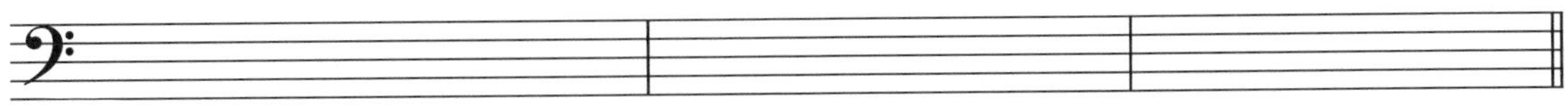

up to F minor

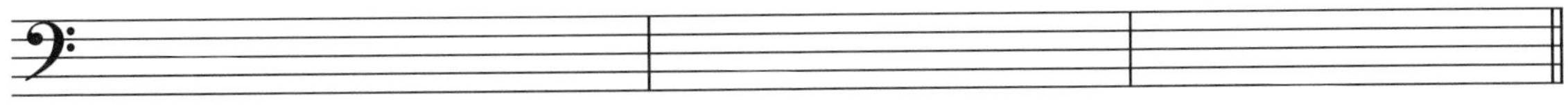

12 Give the name of each chord, with both position in key and root and quality. Identify the cadences as either half cadences or full cadences.

13 On a separate sheet of manuscript paper, develop the following motives into two-phrase melodies. Sing your melodies.

a.

b.

c.

d.

e.

f.

g.

h.

i. lydian mode

j. dorian mode

Harmonize the following melodies (#14–#17). They will need careful consideration and experimentation. Spend some time playing each melody before you begin to choose chords. You may wish to work out several versions on manuscript paper.

14   Choose a harmonic background for this melody. Write an accompaniment.

15 Choose a harmonic background for this melody. Write an accompaniment. Analyze the melody for phrase and cadence. Note that the melody does not end on the tonic.

Appalachian traditional

Key: A major

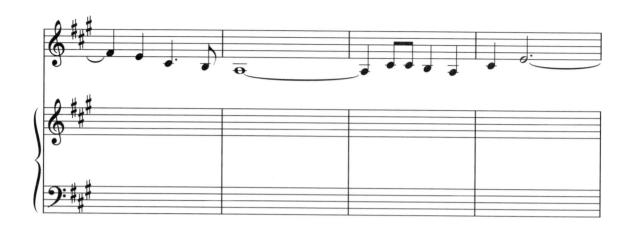

16 Choose a harmonic background for this melody. Write an accompaniment. Analyze for phrase, cadence, motive, and phrase design.

Renaissance English

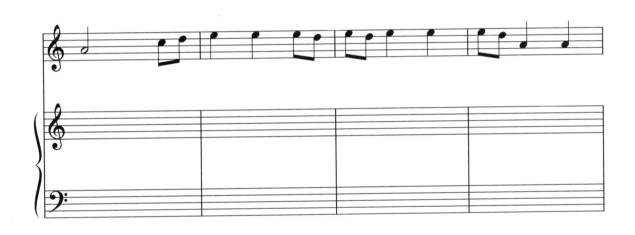

17 Choose a harmonic background for this melody. Compose an accompaniment.

Renaissance English

Appendix I

CHECKLIST OF NOTATION SYMBOLS

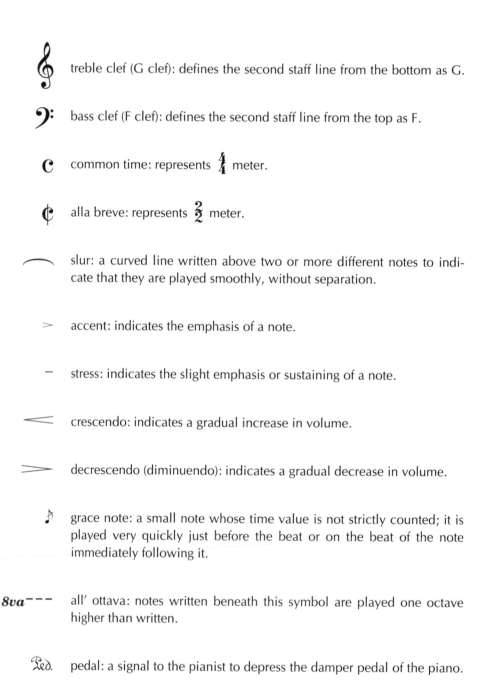

treble clef (G clef): defines the second staff line from the bottom as G.

bass clef (F clef): defines the second staff line from the top as F.

common time: represents $\frac{4}{4}$ meter.

alla breve: represents $\frac{2}{2}$ meter.

slur: a curved line written above two or more different notes to indicate that they are played smoothly, without separation.

accent: indicates the emphasis of a note.

stress: indicates the slight emphasis or sustaining of a note.

crescendo: indicates a gradual increase in volume.

decrescendo (diminuendo): indicates a gradual decrease in volume.

grace note: a small note whose time value is not strictly counted; it is played very quickly just before the beat or on the beat of the note immediately following it.

8va --- all' ottava: notes written beneath this symbol are played one octave higher than written.

Ped. pedal: a signal to the pianist to depress the damper pedal of the piano.

✽ pedal release: a signal to the pianist to release the damper pedal.

tr , ∿   trill: a musical ornament consisting of a rapid alternation between the written note and the note above it.

⌢   fermata: indicates that the note beneath (or above) it should be held longer than its normal duration.

‖: :‖   repeat signs: the music enclosed within these signs is to be performed twice.

ff   fortissimo: very loud.

f   forte: loud.

mf   mezzoforte: moderately loud.

mp   mezzopiano: moderately soft.

p   piano: soft.

pp   pianissimo: very soft.

rit.   ritardando: gradually becoming slower.

Appendix II

MAJOR AND MINOR SCALES AND KEY SIGNATURES

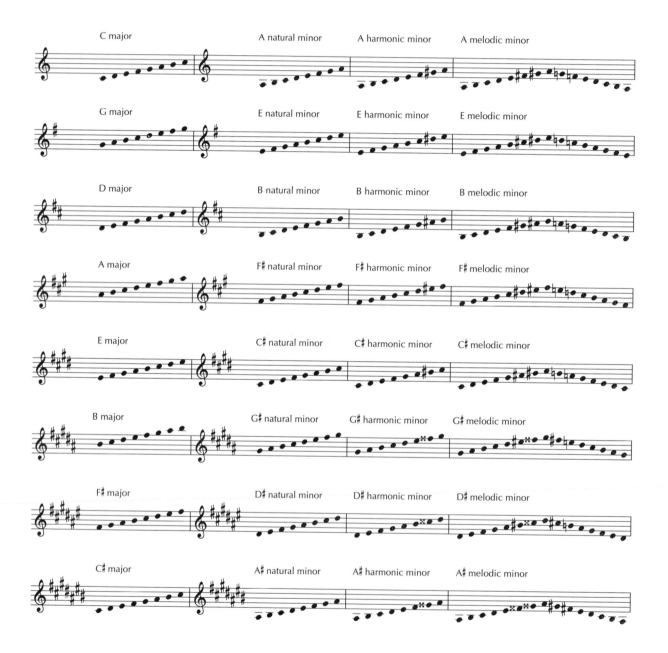

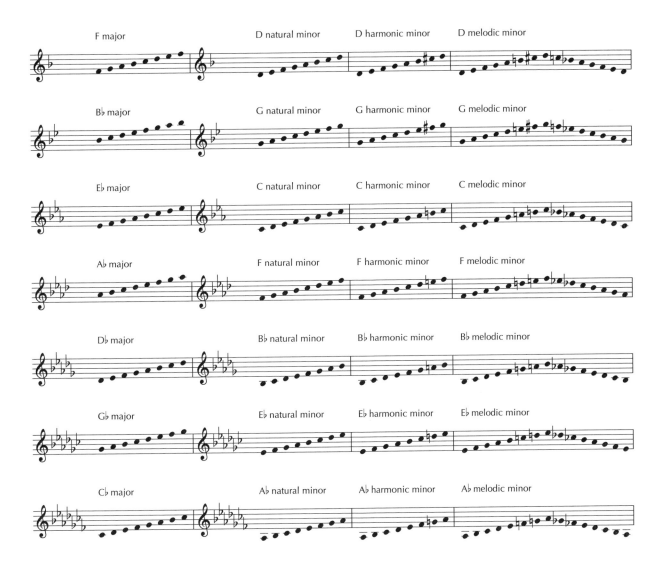

Appendix III

METHODS OF SIGHT SINGING

Fixed *do*: in the fixed *do* system, *each pitch* has only one syllable name. For example, *do* is always C, *re* is always D, and so forth, no matter what major or minor scale is used.

do   di   re   ri   mi   fa   fi   sol   si   la   li   ti   do   ti   te   la   le   sol   se   fa   mi   me   re   ra   do

Movable *do*: in the movable *do* system, syllables apply to *scale degrees*. Therefore, in the key of C major, C is *do* and G is *sol*. In the key of F♯ major, F♯ is *do* and C♯ is *sol*, etc. Note the following variation of syllable names in the major scale and its relative minor:

		do	*re*	*mi*	*fa*	*sol*	*la*	*ti*	*do*
C major	scale degree:	1	2	3	4	5	6	7	8

		do	*re*	*me*	*fa*	*sol*	*le*	*te*	*do*
A natural minor	scale degree:	1	2	3	4	5	6	7	8

Since the 3rd, 6th, and 7th degrees of the natural minor scale are one half step lower than their counterparts in the relative major scale, the syllables are changed to reflect this difference. The same reasoning applies to the harmonic and melodic minor scales:

		do	*re*	*me*	*fa*	*sol*	*le*	*ti*	*do*
A harmonic minor	scale degree:	1	2	3	4	5	6	7	8

		do	*re*	*me*	*fa*	*sol*	*la*	*ti*	*do*	*te*	*le*	*sol*	*fa*	*me*	*re*	*do*
A melodic minor	scale degree:	1	2	3	4	5	6	7	8	7	6	5	4	3	2	1

Reminder: In movable *do*, the tonic scale degree of any major or minor scale is always *do*. (The C major and A minor scales above are examples only.)

Appendix IV

TRIADS AND CHORDS

The following are the most commonly used triads and 7th chords. Although this listing is by no means comprehensive, it includes the chords you will most often encounter.

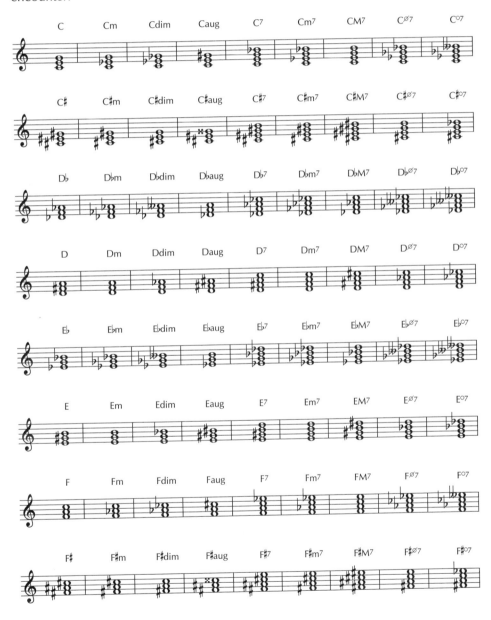

Appendix V

PROGRESSIONS FOR IMPROVISATION AND COMPOSITION

The chord progressions below are suggestions for your own compositions. You may use these progressions to write chord melodies, as points of departure for original pieces, or for improvisation. If you find that a part of one of the progressions appeals to you, use that part and complete it in your own way. Before you begin working with each progression, play it through and listen to it carefully. The brackets indicate possible phrase groupings.

1. Key: C

    C   F   C   G   C   F   G   C

2. Key: D

    D   A   D   G   D   G   A   D

3. Key: D minor

    Dm   Am   Dm   Gm   Dm   Gm   A   Dm

4. Key: C minor

    Cm   Fm   Cm   G   Cm   Fm   Cm   Gm   Cm

5. Key: C

    C   Gm   F   C   Gm   F   B♭   C

6. Key: D

    D   F♯m G   A   Em   Bm   D   A   D

7. Key: D

    D   G   F♯m Bm   D   A   C   G   Bm   Em   A   D

8. Key: F

F   Gm⁷ A⁷ Dm Gm⁷ F   C   F

9. Key: G

G B⁷ Em G⁷   C Bm A⁷ Am⁷ D⁷   Bm Em B⁷ Em   G D⁷ G

10. Key: C minor

Cm Fm Cm B♭   E♭   Fm   C   G⁷   C

11. Key: D minor

Dm G   Dm G   B♭   F   Am   D (major)

12. Key: A minor

Am C   Dm F   Am C   Dm E⁷   Am C   Dm F   Am E⁷ Am

13. Key: B minor

Bm F♯m Em F♯   Bm E   F♯m Bm

14. Key: A

A   A⁷   D⁷   F⁷   B⁷   E⁷   A⁷

15. Key: C

C   B♭   F   Gm⁷ C   Gm B♭   C

16. Key: E

E⁷   G♯⁷ C♯m E⁷   A   E   F♯⁷ B⁷   E⁷

17. Key: C

CM⁷ FM⁷ CM⁷ Gm⁷ F⁷   E♭⁷   B♭⁷   CM⁷

18. Key: A minor

Am F⁷ Am E⁷   Am D⁷ F⁷   Am

19. Key: B♭

B♭M⁷ Dm⁷ E♭M⁷ B♭M⁷ A♭⁷   G♭⁷   E⁷   F⁷   Dm⁷   E♭⁷   Dm⁷   G⁷   Cm⁷   G♭⁷   C♭M⁷ B♭M⁷

20. Key: G

G   B♭⁷   C⁷   G   Em⁷   B⁷   G⁷   C⁷   G   G♯°⁷   Am⁷   E♭⁷   Bm⁷   B♭⁷   Daug G

Appendix VI

HOW TO READ A LEAD SHEET

Popular music is often notated on **lead sheets**, a type of musical shorthand in which only the melody, harmony, and lyrics (if any) are indicated. Performers use the information provided in the lead sheet as the basis for their improvisation. Among the chord name abbreviations and symbols in current use for the key of C are the following:

C	=	C major
Cm	=	C minor
C7	=	C dominant seventh
Cm7	=	C minor seventh
CM7	=	C major seventh
Csus4	=	C suspended fourth

Examples

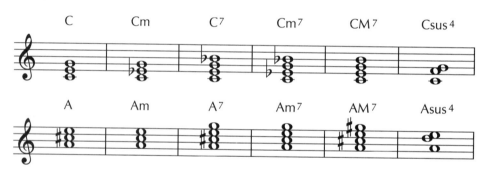

The root of the chord is always used as the bass note *unless* another note is indicated together with the chord name. C/G, for example, indicates a C-major chord played over the bass note G.

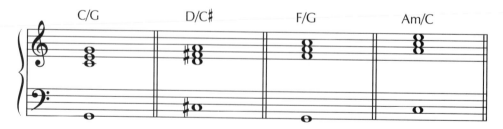

Notes may be added to a chord:

The harmonic rhythm (chord changes) is indicated by the position of the chord designation in relation to the melody or measure. If no chord name appears over a measure, the chord from the previous measure is continued.

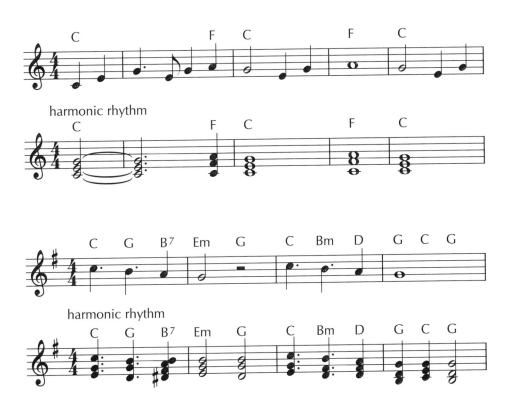

It is up to the performer to choose the rhythm, register (choice of octave), and melodic patterns (sometimes called licks). A specific rhythm or melodic pattern may be indicated in the lead sheet in small notes.

Examples:

3.   Melody and accompaniment from a single-line lead sheet:

melody (sung or played on another instrument)

There are countless possibilities in the realization of a lead sheet. It is interesting to hear how two musicians interpret the same musical outline. Each one brings to the music his or her own style and sound. In popular music, the performer is often a composer as well.

Appendix VII

THE GUITAR FRETBOARD AND GUITAR CHORDS

Guitar Fretboard

fret number	E	A	D	G	B	E	
1	F	A#/Bb	D#/Eb	G#/Ab	C	F	low
2	F#/Gb	B	E	A	C#/Db	F#/Gb	
3	G	C	F	A#/Bb	D	G	
4	G#/Ab	C#/Db	F#/Gb	B	D#/Eb	G#/Ab	
5	A	D	G	C	E	A	
6	A#/Bb	D#/Eb	G#/Ab	C#/Db	F	A#/Bb	
7	B	E	A	D	F#/Gb	B	
8	C	F	A#/Bb	D#/Eb	G	C	
9	C#/Db	F#/Gb	B	E	G#/Ab	C#/Db	
10	D	G	C	F	A	D	
11	D#/Eb	G#/Ab	C#/Db	F#/Gb	A#/Bb	D#/Eb	
12	E	A	D	G	B	E	
13	F	A#/Bb	D#/Eb	G#/Ab	C	F	
14	F#/Gb	B	E	A	C#/Db	F#/Gb	
15	G	C	F	A#/Bb	D	G	
16	G#/Ab	C#/Db	F#/Gb	B	D#/Eb	G#/Ab	
17	A	D	G	C	E	A	high
18	A#/Bb	D#/Eb	G#/Ab	C#/Db	F	A#/Bb	

Guitar Chords

Diagrams are used to indicate the position of the fingers to form chords. The left-hand fingers are numbered 1 to 4 (index to pinky). The thumb is rarely used to form chords.

A number above a string identifies which finger to use in the indicated fret:

3

The diagram above indicates that the third finger is to play in the fourth fret of the fifth string.

An "X" over a string indicates that the string is not played. A "0" indicates that the string is to be played, although it is not fingered. A "(0)" indicates that playing the string is optional.

Below are the guitar fingerings for some frequently used chords.

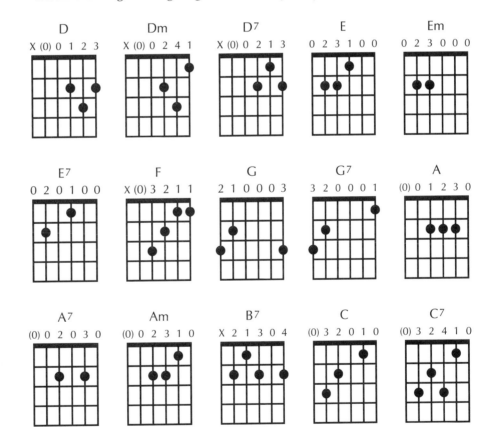

Appendix VIII

RECORDER FINGERING

In the following fingerings for the soprano recorder,

- ○ indicates an open hole;
- ● indicates a closed hole;
- ◐ indicates a hole half closed with the thumb.

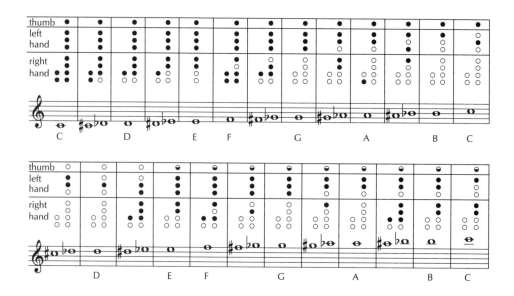

Appendix IX

HARMONIC SERIES

The harmonic series, also called the overtone series, reflects a universal principle of nature. As basic to sound as gravity is to motion, it involves many interrelated phenomena, among them the following:

1. A medium produces a musical tone (for example, a string or a column or air) by *vibrating in parts*.

2. Although we hear a musical tone as having one pitch, it is actually a combination of a **fundamental tone** with many **partial tones** (called partials or overtones).

3. The most prominent tone we hear—the **fundamental**—is the lowest, and is created by the longest and slowest vibrating part (for example, the full length of the string).

4. The **partials** or **overtones** are less audible and are created by shorter and faster vibrating parts.

5. The various parts of the vibrating medium arrange themselves naturally in proportions that can be represented by a **number series**:

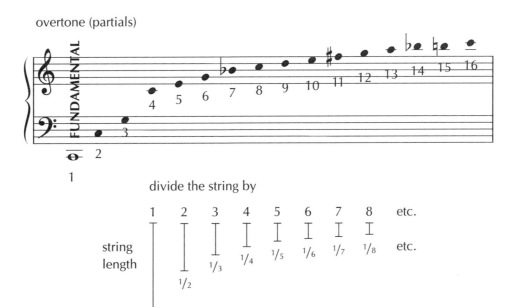

6. **Timbre**, the sound quality of a particular instrument or voice, results from various combinations of overtones, affected by the vibrating medium and the shape and structure of the musical instrument.

Appendix X

GLOSSARY OF TERMS

Words appearing in **bold face** in the definitions are themselves defined in the glossary.

accidentals   Symbols used to raise or lower the pitch of a given note.

alla breve (¢)   A **tempo** marking that indicates fast double time. The half note is the basic pulse.

anacrusis   The **note** or notes that occur at the beginning of a piece on a **beat** other than the first. Sometimes called an **upbeat**.

arpeggio   The **notes** or a **chord** played separately rather than together.

bar line   A vertical line that separates music into **measures**.

bass clef (𝄢, also called the *F clef*)   A symbol written on the staff to identify the second line from the top as F below middle C. Used primarily for the notation of pitches that lie below middle C.

beam   A heavy horizontal line used to join together a group of **notes** smaller than the quarter note.

beat   The basic rhythmic pulse of music.

cadence   A point of rest usually at the end of a phrase or a piece.

canon (popular name, *round*)   A **polyphonic** piece in which the voice parts perform the same material but begin at different times.

chord   Three or more different **pitches** sounding at the same time.

chord tone   One of the **pitches** of a particular chord in a **harmonic progression**.

chromatic scale   A **scale** made up entirely of successive **half steps**.

circle of 5ths   The graphic representation of all the **keys** with their **sharps** and **flats**.

common time (𝄴)   Four-quarter time.

common tone   A **pitch** that remains constant in a voice part while the **harmony** changes.

compound meter   A meter whose basic pulse is regularly divided into three equal parts.

consonance   Musical sound considered to be stable and nonactive. The term is commonly used to describe the agreeable effect of certain **intervals** (**octave**, **3rd**, etc.).

contrasting period   A **period** in which the two **phrases** start differently from one another.

da capo (*D.C.*)   Literally, "from the head." A term that directs the performer to go back to the beginning of the piece. The end is marked *fine*.

dal segno (*D.S.*)   Literally, "from the sign." A term that directs the performer to go back to a point in the piece marked with the sign 𝄋.

diatonic scales   A group of seven-note **scales** containing five **whole steps** and two **half steps** in various fixed relationships and notated with consecutive letter names.

dissonance   Musical sound considered to be unstable and active. The term is commonly used to describe the jarring or disagreeable effect of certain **intervals** (2nd, 7th, etc.).

dominant   The 5th **scale degree**. The *dominant chord* (V) is built on this note.

dorian mode   A medieval church **mode** that may be recreated by playing D to the D an octave higher on the white **keys** of the piano.

dotted note   A **note** with a dot after it; the dot extends the duration of the note by half its own value.

double bar   Two vertical lines indicating the end of a section or piece.

double flat (♭♭)   A symbol that lowers the **pitch** of a **note** a **whole step**.

double period   Two **periods**, separated by a **half cadence**, that balance each other.

double sharp (x)   A symbol that raises the **pitch** of a **note** a **whole step**.

doubling   The practice of giving the same **chord tone** to more than one voice part.

enharmonic   Characterizing **pitches** that sound the same but are notated differently.

F clef   See ***bass clef***.

fermata   A pause, indicated by the sign ⌒.

5th   1. The distance in **pitch** between **diatonic scale degrees** 1 and 5.
2. The uppermost member of a **root-position triad**.

first inversion   The rearrangement of a **chord** so that its **3rd** is in the lowest position.

flag   A curved line drawn on the **stem** of the **note** to identify **notes** smaller than a quarter note.

flat (♭)   A symbol that lowers the **pitch** of a **note** a **half step**.

form   The underlying design and structure of a composition.

full cadence   A **harmonic progression** from V to I that suggests conclusion.

G clef   See ***treble clef***.

grand staff (also called ***great staff*** or ***piano staff***)   The **staffs** of the **treble clef** and the **bass clef** joined with a bracket or brace. The grand staff is used for notating music in all registers.

half cadence   A point of rest on a **chord** other than I, which seems incomplete and creates a desire for additional music.

half step (also called ***semitone*** or ***m2***)   The smallest written **interval** in traditional Western music.

harmonic minor scale   The **scale** resulting from the alteration of the **natural minor** by raising the 7th **scale degree** a **half step**.

harmonic progression   A group of **chords** upon which a **melody** or a piece is based; sometimes called *harmonic background*.

harmonic rhythm   The rhythmic pattern provided by changes of **harmony**.

harmonization   The practice of adding suitable **chords** to a **melody**.

harmony   The vertical structure resulting when two or more pitches or lines of music sound simultaneously.

imitation   The repetition of the same **melody** or **motive** in different voice parts.

interval   The distance in **pitch** between two **notes**.

inversion   1. A **chord** whose lowest **note** is not the **root**.

2. An **interval** whose **notes** have been interchanged.

3. The development of a **motive**, melodic fragment, or **melody** whose ascending or descending direction has been reversed.

key   1. The term used to describe the main **note** or *tonal center* of a piece.

2. In keyboard, woodwind, or brass instruments, the lever depressed by the fingers.

key center   The main **key** around which a piece or section of music revolves.

key signature   The group of **sharps** or **flats** written at the beginning of each **staff** line to indicate required alterations of the **pitches** that form the **scale** and **key** of the piece.

leading tone   The 7th **scale degree** when it is a **half step** lower than the **tonic**.

ledger lines   Lines written above or below the **staff** to extend its range. They are used for notating **pitches** that are too high or low to be written on the **staff**.

lower neighbor   A **nonchord tone** that results when a voice part moves stepwise down and then returns to a **chord tone**.

lydian mode   A medieval church **mode** that may be recreated by playing F to the F an octave higher on the white **keys** of the piano.

major scale   The **diatonic scale** most frequently used in Western music.

measure   A group of **beats** enclosed within **bar lines**, with the first beat usually stressed or accented.

melodic goal   The definite high or low point in a musical line.

melodic minor scale   The **scale** that results when the **natural minor scale** is altered by raising the 6th and 7th **scale degrees** a half step when ascending and lowering them to the original pitches when descending.

melodic shape   The direction and contour of a **melody**.

melody (popular name, *tune*)   A succession of **pitches** that forms a recognizable unit.

meter   A pattern of fixed **beats**; also the number and value of those beats in a **measure**.

minor scale   Related to the **major scale**, and widely used in Western music. It has three forms: **natural**, **harmonic**, and **melodic**.

mixolydian mode   A medieval church **mode** that may be recreated by playing G to the G an octave higher on the white **keys** of the piano.

modal music   Music based on the medieval church **modes** rather than on the **major** or **minor scales**.

mode   A term generally referring to the **diatonic scales** of the medieval church, which may be performed on the white **keys** of the piano.

modulation   The shift to a new **key center** within a piece.

monophonic   Characterizing music consisting of one **melody** only.

motive   A short melodic idea whose **rhythm** and **pitch** designs serve as a basis for a **melody** or piece.

motivic development   The compositional technique of exploring the different characteristics and potentialities of a **motive**.

natural semitones   E to F and B to C, the only **semitones** that do not require **sharps** or **flats**.

natural minor scale   The unaltered **diatonic** form of the **minor scale**.

natural sign (♮)   A sign that cancels the effect of a previous **sharp** or **flat**.

neighbor tone   A **nonchord tone** that moves stepwise from a **chord tone** and immediately returns to it.

nonchord tone   A pitch that does not fit into the *harmonic background*.

note   The written symbol of a musical **pitch**.

notehead   The rounded part of the **note** written on a line or space to indicate **pitch**.

octave   1. The **interval** separating two **pitches** of the same name.
          2. The 8th **note** of a **diatonic scale**.

parallelism   The movement of two or more voice parts in the same direction and at the same intervallic distance from each other.

parallel keys   **Major** and **minor keys** whose **scales** begin on the same **pitch** but have different **key signatures**.

parallel period   A **period** in which both **phrases** begin the same way.

passing tone   A **nonchord tone** that results when a voice part moves stepwise from one **chord tone** to another.

pentatonic scale   A five-note **scale** upon which many of the world's folk songs are based.

period   A two-phrase melodic unit in which the second **phrase** completes the musical thought started by the first.

phrase   A unit of **melody** comparable to a sentence in prose.

phrase design   The relationship of **phrases** within a composition.

phrygian mode   A medieval church **mode** that may be recreated by playing E to the E an octave higher on the white **keys** of the piano.

piano staff   See *grand staff*.

pitch   The highness or lowness of a musical sound depending on its rate of vibration.

polyphonic   Characterizing music consisting of two or more equally important musical lines or melodies that sound at the same time.

quality   The measurement by which we distinguish
          1. **Intervals** of the same number.
          2. **Chords** with the same **root**.

relative major   The term used to identify the **major key** and **scale** having the same **key signature** as its related **minor key** and **scale**. The **relative major** begins on the 3rd **scale degree** of its **relative minor scale**.

relative minor   The term used to identify the **minor key** and **scale** having the same **key signature** as its related **major key** and **scale**. The **relative minor** begins on the 6th **scale degree** of its **relative major scale**.

repeat sign (‖: :‖)   Symbols used to indicate that the music between them should be played again.

repetition   The reiteration of a musical idea.

resolution   The movement of a dissonant sound to a consonant one; the **dissonance** resolves to a **consonance**.

rest   A symbol that indicates the absence of sound for a fixed duration.

rhythm   The organization of music in time.

root   The **note** upon which a **chord** is built.

root position   The arrangement of a **chord** with the root in the lowest position.

round   See *canon*.

scale   A group of **pitches** arranged in ascending or descending order, upon which **melodies** and compositions are based.

scale degrees   The individual notes of a seven-note **scale**, numbered from 1 to 7.

second inversion   The rearrangement of a **chord** so that its **5th** is in the lowest position.

semitone   See *half step*.

sequence   The repetition of a musical pattern on a different **pitch**.

7th chord   A four-note **chord** built in **3rds**.

sharp (♯)   A symbol that raises the **pitch** of a note a **half step**.

simple meter   A **meter** whose basic pulse is regularly divided into two equal parts.

slur   A curved line connecting a group of **notes** to be played smoothly.

staff   The five lines upon which **notes** are written to indicate their **pitch**.

stem   A vertical line drawn to the head of all **notes** smaller than the whole note.

syncopation   Accents off the **beat**.

tempo   The rate of speed of the basic pulse.

3rd   1. The **interval** comprised by two **notes** on adjacent lines or spaces of the **staff**.
    2. The middle member of a **root-position triad**.

tone   A sound of definite pitch.

tonic   The 1st **scale degree**. The *tonic chord* (I) is built on this note.

treble clef (𝄞, also called the *G clef*)   The symbol that indicates that the second line from the bottom of the **staff** is G above middle C. Used primarily to notate pitches that lie above middle C.

triad   A three-note **chord** built in **3rds**.

triplet   A grouping of three successive **notes** performed in the time usually allotted to two.

upbeat (also called *anacrusis*)   The **note** or notes that occur at the beginning of a piece on a **beat** other than the first.

upper neighbor   A **nonchord tone** that results when a voice part moves stepwise up and then returns to a **chord tone**.

variation   A new musical version of a preexisting musical idea.

voice leading   The principles governing the movement of separate voice parts in harmonic progressions.

whole step (also called *whole tone* or *M2*)   An **interval** consisting of two **half steps**.